PRAISE FOR
Potluck Culture

"Well written, powered by true stories, and rich with a plethora of tangible and practical action plans and step-by-step guidance, *Potluck Culture* may very well be the best book written on organizational culture. Dr. Nair is clearly well versed in systems thinking. He recognizes what organizations are made of (people, processes, technologies, value systems, relationships, motivational factors, and so on). His book is the best recipe for leaders who are systems thinkers and are determined to bring about organizational success through collaboration and synergistic teamwork."

— **Dr. Bijan Masumian, Manager, Learning & Development, Advanced Micro Devices, Austin, TX**

"Dr. Ranjit Nair has created essentially a new textbook containing all of the most critical aspects of organizational culture that C-suite executives and HR professionals will be using as a key reference for years to come. And he does it in 163 pages and a few appendices, which makes it much easier to use as a working handbook guiding the process of organizational development and culture building. Ranjit's broad experience and profound depth in all topics relevant to HR, in the best sense as people development, is evident throughout the book. I sincerely think every leader of every organization and every HR director needs to have this book, highlight it, apply it, and buy another copy after it's worn out. It's that good!"

— **Andy Johnson, Leadership Coach and Author of** *Introvert Revolution: Leading Authentically in a World that Says You Can't,* **Boise, ID**

"People support what they help to create. *Potluck Culture* provides five key strategies allowing every employee to contribute breakthrough improvements in their company's culture. Dr. Nair makes it possible to accelerate the journey of change with a simple and straightforward approach."

— **Chris McSwain, Chief Strategy Officer, Aasonn, Naperville, IL**

Potluck CULTURE

Five Strategies to Engage the Modern Workplace

Ranjit Nair Ph.D.

Potluck Culture: Five Strategies to Engage the Modern Workplace
by Ranjit Nair Ph.D. © 2015

Print ISBN: 978-1-61206-111-5
eBook ISBN: 978-1-61206-112-2

Interior and Cover Design by: Fusion Creative Works, www.fusioncw.com
Editing Team: Kim Foster, Stacy Ennis, Jennifer Regner

For more information, visit www.ranjitnairphd.com

Published by

AlohaPublishing.com

First Printing
Printed in the United States of America
First Edition
2 4 6 8 10 12

This is my first book and it is dedicated to my parents—Mrs. Sathi B. Nair and Mr. P.S.B. Nair—who were married for fifty-three years and made everything possible for me. My father, who was a high school teacher for forty years and never forgot a face, name, or any one of his students, passed away the year after I received my doctorate. He was present and listened as I delivered the oral defense of my doctoral research. After I finished my presentation—normally the culmination of the rigorous doctoral journey—he pulled me aside and said, "Son, this is one of the proudest days of my life. Now go and make it count."

ABOUT THE AUTHOR

Ranjit Nair Ph.D. is a speaker, author, advisor and educator. In his role as a Senior Strategist with Price Associates and lead facilitator for The Complete Leader, he works with senior executives to implement a "potluck culture" where everyone brings their best to the table to create a culture of shared success.

As a former talent management executive, Dr. Nair has unique insight and the ability to act as a bridge between both traditional and new thinking about talent development. He helps companies maneuver challenges in organizational development, talent management, talent acquisition, compensation and benefits, succession planning, change management, organizational culture, performance management, and executive development.

As a noted global business expert, Dr. Nair works with companies that are engaged in Asia, Europe and the U.S. His experience in global business includes global human capital management and organizational effectiveness, strategic leadership, functional oversight, and cultural inculcation. Dr. Nair has worked at marquis global organizations in senior human resource management roles including

Bank of America, Honeywell International, Becton Dickinson, and PriceWaterhouseCoopers, and was the chief human resource officer at Globalfoundries.

Dr. Nair received his Ph.D. from Capella University in Organization and Management.

He is a Certified Six Sigma Black Belt, Certified Compensation Professional and Certified Change Integrator™. He also holds a Certificate in Strategic Human Resource Management from Harvard Business School and a Senior Professional Human Resources certification. He is a member of the Society for Human Resource Management (SHRM), World-at-Work, and the Academy of Management.

Together with his wife, Jiji, a nutritionist and wellness coach, Dr. Nair lives in Boise with his son, Nikhil, daughter, Nikita, and their labradoodle, Ziggy. When he's not traveling and meeting new people, he enjoys golf, yoga, and soccer.

Contents

Chapter 1

THE POTLUCK CULTURE

"Success in business is all about people, people, and people.
Whatever industry a company is in, its employees are
its biggest competitive advantage."

—Richard Branson, founder, Virgin Group

When I was growing up in Hong Kong, I spent the summers with my family vacationing in India where I was born. These summers were full of joy and fascination for me, learning Indian language and culture, appreciating the ways people lived, and experiencing the ups and downs of growing up. During those formative days, I spent a lot of time with my grandmother, the matriarch of the family and also a farmer. It was quite unusual in those days for a female farmer to own her own land. She and I were inseparable, and I looked to her as my first true mentor and sage.

My grandmother was also a phenomenal storyteller. My brothers, cousins, and even the neighborhood children would regularly gather around her and listen to stories about life, growing up, our neighborhood and community, and the epic stories and parables about Hindu mythology, such as the Bhagavad-Gita and the Ramayana.

She'd spent most of her life learning how to make her farm prosperous while building deep and lasting relationships with everyone with whom she interacted. This included her handful of employees, poor and underprivileged transients just looking for a wholesome meal in exchange for hard work, and all of the vendors and merchants in the small ecosystem in the southern Indian village where she lived. To her, *everyone* mattered and it was obvious that she had a wonderful way with people.

One hot and humid day, we were sitting together, looking out over the rice paddies and farm fields. We had been talking about the mundane things in life—nothing I can really even remember today. But I do vividly recall what happened next.

My grandmother grew silent. She turned and looked at me with her kind and wise eyes. "My dear son," she began, "if you want to have one year of prosperity, grow rice. If you want ten years of prosperity, grow orchards. And if you want a hundred years of prosperity, develop relationships and grow people." She went on to talk about how every life matters and everyone brings something of value that can benefit someone else.

How prophetic she was! For many years after that, she repeated that message, making sure I never forgot that relationships—people—are what really matter. While these powerful words had little meaning to me then, it wasn't until she passed away when I was in my early forties that I realized the impact of what she had told me. At her funeral—held at the same old farm she had owned and loved—over two thousand people showed up in that village to bid their adieus to her.

All of those people she had interacted with during her life—including those she had given some work to do in exchange for food—didn't forget her and returned to say farewell. Many had traveled hundreds of miles just to pay their respects.

Today, people are the center of my entire life.

As a business strategist, I help organizations realize what they need aren't necessarily new logos, cool websites, revamped mission statements or modern strategic business approaches. Rather, they are often in need of a renewed vision and authentic focus on people. This organizational *attitude adjustment* must be honest and genuine and executed with a deep, meaningful, and even *maniacal* focus on their greatest assets—people.

All people management strategies concern people. However, in today's workplace, the focus of most of these strategies is invariably on the business and usually targeted at the paying customer. Old adages such as "the customer is always right" and "customer first" still hold true, but to achieve them, organizations must focus on *who* makes this level of service, commitment and loyalty happen. Many leaders minimize or underappreciate that people in the organization are the very resources that enable them to achieve these objectives.

Most organizations say great things publicly about their appreciation of people. Leaders profess how proud they are of their teams. Some organizations even declare on their company Internet sites that it's their people who bring them success. Others go further, asserting that they've unlocked the value of their people in enabling business success through teamwork and collaboration and honor them through success stories and anecdotes. They speak of how their people, then, have delighted paying customers.

However, very few organizations truly value their people once behind the comfortable, safe—and closed—confines of their respective workplaces.

Experienced organizational leaders need to radically and quickly reform their workplaces because inauthenticity and complacency abound today. Does your organization really have a people-focused culture? Do you know how to build one? Do you know how to get the best out of your people to enable shared success—profitability for the company and career enhancement for employees?

I wrote *Potluck Culture* to help leaders think about, understand, and authentically appreciate people in their organizations. By doing so, they will liberate and then engage their greatest competitive advantage—people—and transform the workplace to drive profitability and strategic success. To help bring these concepts to life, I tell the true stories of real people who try hard to succeed and of those who help them succeed. I also draw from my experience as a talent manager, human resources (HR) and business leader, and from the rights and wrongs that I witnessed, participated in, and even predicted.

As a twenty-five-year veteran of the global workforce, I've discovered that by giving people the opportunity, they will bring their best to the table. To help people do so, I recommend that leaders adopt five key strategies: get the right fit, build a culture of dialogue, motivate with purpose, innovate as a habit, and make work meaningful. And it all starts with fostering what I call a Potluck Culture. Given the opportunity, everyone brings something to the table.

The Potluck Culture

Over the years, I've attended and even sponsored numerous events where the meeting theme was conducted around a potluck feast. Yes, potluck—a food fest. You've surely been to some kind of food fest in your life, likely even a workplace potluck.

At each one of the workplace potluck gatherings I've enjoyed, I can recall a sense of camaraderie, a coming together of different mindsets and walks of life. Interesting, meaningful and well-intentioned conversations took place where, literally, people brought their best to the table. Of course, usually there was a plethora of fine food, brought by meeting attendees from all around the world. Many just showed up for the food but found much to be gained from the mingling of cultures and perspectives, as well as the richness and diversity of the dialogue that flourish in such settings.

Potlucks are about *sharing*. People—in this case, people at the workplace—sharing a space, stories, food, and company, and just getting to know one another. This philosophy is a part of food cultures all over the world and can easily be used as a metaphor for workplace cultures that honor and respect people.

Potluck Culture:

A wholesome workplace where employees are engaged;
managers are in sync with how to build and develop their teams;
leaders are inspiring and behave as role models; and customers are
satisfied, delighted and, most of all, captivated. All of the ingredients of
a great potluck gathering make for a phenomenal Potluck Culture.

POTLUCK CULTURE

Have you ever noticed there is less small talk at potlucks than most other company gatherings? That's because everyone wants to talk about food and cooking! People want to brag about how they not only made the avocado dip from scratch, but they also grew the ingredients that went into it. If you happen to make a particularly wonderful dish, you never know who might seek you out to ask for the recipe. This type of connecting with others can result in long-term relationships that will only help companies succeed. There can even be healthy competition about who made the best dish or who deserves recognition for their tireless efforts. When applied metaphorically to the concept of a Potluck Culture, such competition in a workplace serves the company well, leading to teamwork, greater motivation, collaboration, and ideation.

At a potluck, everyone is the cook, host and guest; there is a sense of community without any hierarchy or division of roles. Everyone is empowered irrespective of title, level, tenure, or role in the company. Everyone does the dishes, cleans up after the gathering, and puts the furniture back into place. But everyone gets to eat well and has the chance to show off their skills. There is something magical about this type of dynamic—the Potluck Culture—that companies can study and incorporate into their organizational cultures.

Looking around a potluck gathering, you might notice the varied people, all enjoying the food and conversation. This depth of diversity has never before existed in the modern workplace: race, gender, political affiliations, ideologies, religion, attitudes about work, sexual orientation and experiences. The latter attribute—experience—in itself poses some unprecedented opportunities. The modern workplace is ripe with varying generations, each bringing different delectable nuggets to the table. From Traditionalists to Boomers, Gen Xers and Millennials (Yers) to the new kids on the block, the Gen Zers, the opportunities to truly get the best out of people have never been more available. At the same time, this diversity is daunting and challenging for organizational leaders and their stewards of the workplace, HR professionals.

Potluck Cultures honor people and what they bring to the table. Given the opportunity, all people will rise to the challenge and deliver their best. Yet too often in today's workplace, managers and leaders are preoccupied with structure, process, metrics, and administration. They don't spend enough time doing what is necessary to harness the skills of their most prized assets: their human resources. If done right and with the proper intent, managing talent will result in more highly engaged workers who are aligned tightly to the core and strategic objectives of their companies.

The best leaders are not only authentic, inspirational and visionary, but they also make others better. It is in this vein that a Potluck Culture is most valuable.

It starts with a deep and humble appreciation of all employees—not just management and those labeled "high potentials." Why not have talent management and reverence for *all* employees, regardless of title? Why not enlist all employees willfully and meaningfully to help the organization succeed? Why can't success be determined under the premise of "sharing"? With the Potluck Culture mindset, employees get what they desire and companies receive what they crave.

Leaders typically try to build the concept of "shared values" to bring the organization together. Values such as integrity, teamwork, customer-first, collaboration, and community ring through fancy and colorful websites and adorn company walls. However, these values must be rephrased and repositioned as *shared success*; the focus must be on both the company *and* the individual. Every organization and every <u>leader</u>

needs to appreciate what really drives and motivates employees and then do something meaningful about it.

What Is Shared Success?

Even though employers and employees share the workplace, and may even, arguably, have shared values, there is a real disconnect between their drivers and motivations. Ingrained in the minds of most employers is that employees are hired for a purpose and need to be true to that purpose—to help the company succeed in its strategic imperatives. Organizations often overlook a critical piece: employee engagement.

My work with companies of all sizes and kinds has revealed three types of employees (see Table 1). The more actively engaged the employees, the deeper the connection they feel to the company as a whole and as a part of a Potluck Culture. They feel a responsibility for the success of the organization, and their passion shows in everything they say and do. Who wouldn't want employees like that?

Table 1. The three types of employees

Actively Engaged	These employees have a deep connection to their companies, fellow employees, managers, and leaders and feel passionate about their work. They drive innovation and help their companies succeed.
Somewhat Engaged	These employees include those who have either literally *checked out* but still put in their time, though not with conviction or passion, or those who may still be deciding if the company is the right fit and may eventually be engaged.
Actively Disengaged	These employees are unhappy. They are not engaged, and *worse*, they act it and daily undermine and ridicule what their engaged colleagues accomplish.

In today's complex world, where the line between work and life has blurred, it is critical to have authentic workplaces and people-centered work environments where employees are empowered to lead their own career destiny, engage continually in their work, and collaborate effectively to accomplish goals. As we explored earlier, the workplace of today brings together at least four different generations interacting with one another: Traditionalists, Baby Boomers, Gen Xers, and Millennials (Gen Yers), with Gen Zers on their way in. These employees yearn to be connected with and engaged in the purpose of their employment. They seek careers in workplaces where they are valued, respected, and trusted.

We have evolved into a new age, a focus-on-people age. That's the good news. The challenge—which is also the opportunity—is to help companies and leaders develop their own leadership skills while also training those of the next generation. Organizations that introduce an empathetic and proactive approach to leadership development through talent management and succession planning are planting the seeds of future leadership. These organizations truly take the time to assess and understand their people. The seeds they sow will grow into mature and healthy plants and bear the greatest fruits: motivated, engaged, collaborative, empathetic, and self-aware leaders of the future.

And true to the Potluck Culture, they'll also have engaged employees at every level of employment, from entry level to CEO. There is reciprocity between what the company wants and what employees want, a true environment of shared success (see Figure 1). A workplace with these qualities will take companies to greatness—and make shareholders extremely happy.

Figure 1. Shared success elements

Nothing Comes Easily

In 1961, John F. Kennedy, thirty-fifth president of the United States, spoke to a crowd at Rice University. During his now famous speech, he said,

> We choose to go to the moon in this decade and do the other things, not because they are easy, but because they are hard, because that goal will serve to organize and measure the best of our energies and skills, because that challenge is one that we are willing to accept, one we are unwilling to postpone, and one which we intend to win, and the others, too.

Kennedy's speech can be distilled to a single message: nothing worth achieving comes easily. This concept had a powerful and lasting impact on me as an HR leader and a leader of people in the workplace. I have seen again and again that when organizations do the tough and challenging work of motivating and inspiring people to work hard, people rise to the challenge. They can achieve almost anything.

In a Potluck Culture, leaders who understand their employees enable them to proudly take the company's vision and transform it into their personal stories, in which they play the starring roles. In such a culture, everyone is encouraged to bring their best to the table, allowing them to be more autonomous and trusting of their leaders, more collaborative and purposeful in their work.

One thing that binds people together is a love of challenge. President Kennedy understood this well and worked to build a country that thrived on innovation. He challenged the nation to go where no person had ever gone before—the moon. Whether it is trying to solve a complex crossword puzzle or getting to the ultimate level in one's favorite video game, diving the deepest oceans to film a rare sea creature or climbing Mount Kilimanjaro, people are genuinely inclined to take challenges. Appreciating this as Kennedy did and having a deep desire to help others and allow them to succeed is a powerful combination.

Imagine peeling off the roof of such a workplace and looking inside. Peering down, you see everyone (leaders, managers, and all other employees) speaking positively about the organization to one another, whether informally or as part of a requisite process such as performance management. All employees are experiencing a deep sense of belonging and appreciation, along with an intense desire to be a part of an organization that actively appreciates them. Finally, these motivated employees trust their leaders. Their leaders, in turn, promote each employee's autonomy, which enhances the effort toward success in one's job and for the company. Customers can almost *feel* the authentic environment, where there is a clear sense of belonging, a Potluck Culture.

Such a work world will require a company's culture to be based on respectful dialogue and constructive feedback. It requires employees to have deep trust in management, allowing them to focus on work and not linger on suspicious thoughts of being underpaid and unmotivated or demotivated. This culture has a reverential flow of collaboration and teamwork, which leads to innovation and continued productivity—all conducted by employees who have a sense of belonging and appreciation.

You can have an organization like the one I've described. I will show you strategies for cultivating this type of culture throughout this book, focusing on five key ways to get you to a place of true collaboration. Before we investigate them in detail, let's explore the realities of the workplace and what abounds in it today.

The Drivers

Chapter 2

CHALLENGES FACING THE
MODERN WORKPLACE

"Life throws challenges and every challenge comes
with rainbows and lights to conquer it."

— **Amit Ray, author of** *World Peace:*
The Voice of a Mountain Bird

If employees truly are a company's best and most powerful asset, then
their care and support should be a priority. That priority should be
inextricably tied to its business strategy. According to a 2014 study
conducted by Aon Hewitt, a global human capital consulting firm,
employee engagement around the world's workplaces has continued
to rebound since late 2009, growing to an average of approximately
sixty percent within workforces. In North America, employment engagement levels are around sixty-five percent; Europe is at fifty-seven
percent; Asia, Africa, and the Middle East are at sixty-one percent;
and Latin America (usually the top of the heap) is at seventy percent.[1]

According to the study, increased employee engagement leads to economic stability. This means engaged employees enhance an organiza-

tion's ability to succeed strategically and financially. The study went on to reveal the primary drivers of employee engagement and what truly makes it happen. They are listed in the order of most influential:

1. Career opportunities
2. Feedback on performance
3. Company reputation
4. Pay and rewards
5. Communication
6. Innovation
7. Recognition
8. Brand Alignment

While this list should not come as a surprise to anyone, several note-worthy themes emerged. Career opportunities are genuinely provided only if managers have the right dialogue with employees, especially about their performance, and are transparent about their pay and how it is determined. Most significantly, for today's socially connected world, the company's internal practices should reflect its external image and brand. Employees not only yearn for such a workplace, they demand it.

The challenge is for companies and leaders to make people a priority, even though they may not know the best way to do it. To intensify matters, significant global workforce trends are developing. These trends include a potentially devastating leadership drought brought on mostly by the rise of inexperienced Millennials and fast-retiring Traditionalists and Boomers; a social media movement that can make or break companies who risk their brand through poor people practices; and a need to compete in and ultimately win the talent war.

Company leaders and HR management professionals must heed these ominous trends or risk being left behind.

So, is your company preparing your people to drive performance in the face of these looming realities? The data suggests most are not prepared enough, and many do not have the know-how to implement necessary changes. Business leaders face extraordinary challenges brought on by workforce trends, and only those with a savvy and unfazed people-centric approach will win.

In a Potluck Culture, each one of the engagement drivers is incorporated as part of the organization's business strategy. In other words, having specific strategies to develop career opportunities for people, focus performance management on behavior, provide frequent dialogue between manager and employee, and demystify pay help establish the foundation of a trusting and collaborative environment. As organizations encourage employees to be active in wellness programs, proudly share success stories about people and teams, recognize and reward them accordingly, and respect people through regular communication and interaction, they form the basis of a powerful culture. Executed well, each one of these strategies can mean everything for a company's success.

The Leadership Drought

In both the 2014 and 2015 Deloitte studies,[2] leadership was cited as the top talent issue organizations face today. An overwhelming majority of survey respondents cited it as urgent or important. If you take into consideration the need to develop Millennials, who will be fifty percent of the workforce by 2020,[3] the "gap" created in leadership roles is more like a seismic fissure. Developing this next generation of leaders is crucial, yet very few companies are ready for this challenge.

Companies need to take a different approach to addressing the modern workforce, which is made up of an increasingly global, tech-savvy, interconnected, and diverse people. Organizations are challenged with developing multiple generations of leaders (not just Millennials) with high flexibility and global fluency, and ensuring that leaders have the skills to understand and adapt to rapidly changing technologies. A new perspective is needed. Asking people to sit through PowerPoint presentations and conferences about leadership skills will no longer cut it. Essentially, leadership is taking on a much broader meaning than simply developing the next CEO or company C-Suite executive.

The stark reality facing the modern workplace is that there is and will continue to be a leadership drought. Organizations will soon feel the impact of this change in their recruiting and retention statistics. Each day, ten thousand Baby Boomers reach retirement age. This generation of talent forms the backbone of leadership teams in today's work world. They are the current chief executives, senior managers, and strategy leaders who steer and influence the direction of their companies.

According to Ron Price, the renowned leadership and performance expert, and author of *The Complete Leader*,[4] the challenge is that there are not enough leaders groomed, trained, and ready to replace them. According to the US Department of Labor, by 2020, the number of Baby Boomers in the workplace will be cut from forty percent to approximately twenty percent.[5] In the meantime, Millennials (discussed later in the second workplace trend) will grow from twenty percent to fifty percent of the workforce, while the generation in between (the Xers) is not sufficient in number to fill the leadership gaps about to appear.[6]

CHALLENGES FACING THE MODERN WORKPLACE

Companies must grapple with defining leadership readiness. Leadership involves a whole set of required skills that enables one to lead through a deep sense of self-awareness, empathy, and engagement; make clear, focused decisions; and behave respectfully and authentically. Many companies do not teach these skills effectively or use the right processes. Too many leaders are trained through classroom instruction as opposed to hands-on, experiential learning where they make mistakes and learn from them.

Looking at responses from executives who participated in the Deloitte surveys, more than sixty percent reported believing they were "weak" in their ability to develop Millennial leaders, and just five percent rated themselves as "excellent." Additionally, fifty-one percent of executives had little confidence in their ability to maintain clear, consistent succession programs, and only eight percent felt they had excellent programs to build global skills.[7]

To build a deeper leadership bench and enhance the quality of leadership, you need to assess whether your company is ready and prepared for the looming leadership drought. Under the banner of a Potluck Culture, these fundamental questions must be answered:

1. What *skills* do you need to win in today's marketplace?
2. What *type* of leaders do you want to develop?
3. How do you develop *current* leaders?
4. How will you identify and develop *future* leaders?

In addition to fundamental leadership skills, these leaders need to be resourceful and flexible, globally eloquent and nimble enough to respond to rapidly changing technologies.

Building a culture of authenticity is germane to being people-centric and genuinely interested in the welfare and development of people in the workplace. These are prime issues for all generations of employees, but become significantly more relevant when engaging Millennials—the fastest-rising segment in today's workforce.

The Rise of Millennials

Each of the five generational segments in today's workforce brings life experiences and expectations to the workplace, along with their values and work preferences. Table 2 shows the summary of the values and perspectives of each generation.

Table 2. Projected demographics in 2020[8]

Generation	Percentage of Workforce in 2015	Percentage of Workforce by 2020	Values and Perspectives
Traditionalists	10%	1%	Loyalty; *one* company for life
Baby Boomers	40%	20%	Live to work; focus on learning
Generation X	30%	25%	Work to live; revels in structure
Millennials (Generation Y)	20%	50%	Seek meaning in work; craves constant feedback
Generation Z	1%	5%	Native technologist; inherently connected socially

Organizational leaders are coping with how to manage and lead within this unparalleled workplace dynamic. A cultural paradigm shift in the workplace and true authentic leadership are sorely needed to get the best out of all mindsets—particularly Millennials because they are the newest to the work core and have unique perspectives, preferences and expectations in the modern workplace.

A 2015 PriceWaterhouseCoopers' white paper on Millennial motivations revealed that this new talent cohort, unlike their predecessors, will no longer accept or tolerate the demands of work at the expense of personal or life needs.[9] A young Millennial friend of mine, Chance, whom I met at a seminar where I was speaking, said this to me:

> I am living life and I want to enjoy it. Life is work and work is life. It doesn't consume my entire life and it's just one element of what I do. Fortunately, I work for a company that recognizes me in many ways—one of which is that I cannot commit to making my work life take precedence over my personal life, even with the promise of more pay for performance.

Chance went on to say that he shouldn't be viewed as someone who was lazy or not willing to commit to a company and its strategic priorities. He was ready, willing, and able to put his best foot forward but not willing to compromise the promise of life and its many offerings. When I asked him if his company did anything special to engage him, he said he felt a sense of autonomy because he could work on the things he likes. He had opportunities to learn new skills on projects regularly and also "gets to do cool things," like work on projects that have significant interactions with paying customers.

Millennials are known as idealistic, tech-savvy natives, who constantly want feedback and (in some cases) pose a challenge for older generations to work with. However, in workplaces around the world today, and for the foreseeable future, leaders will be contending with how to maximize the opportunity to engage this new generation of employees.

POTLUCK CULTURE

There are around seventy million Baby Boomers and most of them will be retiring in the next five to ten years. As Boomers and Millennials continue to work side by side, this is an opportunity to enhance this relationship and to end the leadership drought, propel innovation, and delight customers.

Championed by enterprising organizations such as Zappos, Amazon, Intuit, and Google, the skills, knowledge, and wisdom that Boomers have gained from decades of work and their experiences have contributed significantly to the success of these companies by first understanding, then rearing and nurturing Millennials. Together, the older generation and the young upstarts have proven invaluable on complex projects to help these organizations drive change. This experienced core of leaders are trying to find personal meaning in the twilight of their careers and see Millennials as the ideal cast to pass on their wisdom and savvy. This also means more Boomers will be sticking around the office for years to come. Companies need to take advantage of this treasure trove of knowledge and experience to engage the next generation, who sits on the other end of the demographic spectrum.

While each generation wants to leave its unique mark on the workplace, their perspectives vary dramatically. For example, Baby Boomers are more concerned about their immediate personal well-being and are typically late to the retirement planning party. On the other hand, Millennials are starting their retirement planning campaign early and want to have a solid plan in place by age twenty-five.[10]

By 2020, Millennials will form at least fifty percent of the global workforce. They expect to start saving for retirement soon after entering the workforce. More than fifty percent of Millennials say retirement benefits—not necessarily base salary—are very influential in their job choices. It isn't a coincidence that participation rates for company-sponsored 401(k) savings plans are at an unprecedented high since the post-2008's economic downturn. Eighty percent of Millennials contribute to such programs.[11]

Baby Boomers, true to their "let's get work done" attitude, attempt to develop a spirit of camaraderie with team members whose on-the-job experience are zero to none. It is very likely that twenty-somethings are working next to colleagues with an age span of fifty years or even more. Vietnam veterans are taking orders from new managers significantly younger than them. The current stalwarts of the workplace (Gen Xers) are tasked with the unenviable role of developing critical company processes, business operational strategies, and HR policies, and building workplace cultures that will affect the quality of life for colleagues old enough to be their grandparents.

Serendipity—Be Careful What You Ask For

People. That's the answer to most challenges in business. It seems simple, but as I've learned over the years, it can be difficult to shift an entire organization to focus on people first.

It was ironic or maybe a divine intervention—probably my grandmother still looking after me—that one day at work, something changed my career forever. I was a senior consultant at PriceWaterhouseCoopers when I complained about my local HR team. Irritated with their lack of business acumen, under-appreciation for the paying customer, and unnecessary overemphasis on administrative matters, rigid policies and strong-armed policing tactics, I uttered these words to my supervisors, "Will someone fix those idiots in HR?"

HR had been paying lip service to leaders while focusing on administrative matters, as opposed to really understanding people, the skills they possess and their untapped potential. My complaints resulted in an offer by my employers to run the HR function outright.

Dumbfounded, I asked them, "Why me?" To this, they replied, "Because you know us, our business, our customers, and you will find a way to get the best out of our people. We believe in you and feel strongly that you will honor our people as our greatest assets."

At first, I was upset by this notion. Why would I want to work in a function I despised and, frankly, knew very little about? My mentors and superiors at the time explained that it was up to me to make a difference. Since then, I have been a people-centric HR leader, tapping into potential to make a difference in the strategic outcomes of companies.

After twenty years in various leadership roles in the HR function, I left the private sector to teach. It was during three years of teaching at St. Edward's University in Austin, Texas, that I truly got a sense of what a people-centric culture was all about.

A former student of mine, Farhan (a very talented individual in his late twenties) would tell me stories about how he grew up with both of his parents working full time. Both always complained about their workday, their managers, and the monotony and stress of work itself. He grew up hearing horror work stories and didn't want to experience the same thing in his lifetime. He dreaded graduating and finding work but was excited to have a life and be happy as well. So he looked for a job in a company that cared about people and what they brought to the table.

CHALLENGES FACING THE MODERN WORKPLACE

Farhan told me, "When I hear and read about Google culture, I get jazzed because I want to learn, keep learning and, hopefully, continue to love what I do every day." He eventually was hired by Google. Farhan's story is not specific to Millennials. All employees in every company want to be cared for by their employers and taken seriously, and they want to make a difference in that employer's strategic imperatives.

On the other end of the spectrum, one Traditionalist I know well, a Vietnam War veteran named Trevor, told me how it was hard to adapt to a manager almost forty years younger than him. He said, "It was hard at first—well, it's still hard but I am getting the hang of it. I need the job and I work hard trying to follow directions and find meaning in what I do. Taking orders from such a young person has given me a new perspective on who I am." More and more Millennials are entering leadership roles early in their careers and being promoted faster, largely because of their intellect, dedication, and personality. However, to ensure they have the right skills and more importantly, to retain them, requires the existing older core of leaders to step up their managerial game.

Both of these true stories bring light to the fact that we have entered a golden age of leadership potential where a multigenerational workforce, spearheaded by emerging leaders, fuels economic success. Organizations that focus on succession planning and talent management, conduct it well, and actively engage their older generation leaders in the process will survive. Those who are prepared for the leadership drought will have a long-term competitive advantage that ensures longevity and continuity in their businesses for future generations. The key to revitalizing the organization is identifying emerging leaders, honing and sharpening their skills, and thereby preparing them for senior leadership roles.

Employee Engagement

Employee engagement is a commitment to creating
a workplace culture that puts people first.

After all, no organization in the world says they are anti-people, anti-customers, anti-environment, and anti-community. Rather, they typically claim to have values that honor people, revere community, and intensely focus on customers in their pitches via the Internet. However, too many of them often fail miserably to engage their employees and woefully miss the chance to inspire and motivate them. The Millennials will not let them get away with it. They will simply gravitate toward work environments that *do* inspire and motivate them. Therefore, it is imperative to build a proposition that resonates with this new group of thinkers.

Millennials, a generation which accounts for about eighty million individuals, were lauded and praised by their Boomer parents, according to a study conducted by the Pew Research Center.[12] Growing up they were told how smart they were, how good their accomplishments were, and that they could accomplish anything they set their minds on. Accordingly, Millennials crave success and demand recognition for even basic, routine tasks. They relentlessly want to know *why* before they do anything and expect to be consulted on company matters big and small. They see work-life balance as a birthright and want to constantly demonstrate creativity and innovation.

Millennials who have developed leadership potential proactively seek out learning and growth from their older generation, workplace counterparts. Many would rather be taught by their elders than learn on their own. They seek clarity of vision for their company's strategic imperatives first and then look within themselves and to their environment to gauge whether they can be inspired, motivated and unleashed to help make an impact.

A study conducted by PriceWaterhouseCoopers makes claims about the general characteristics of Millennials and how they might respond to the workplace and its environment.[13] It is without a doubt that Millennials will be most engaged when working with people they think are smart, social, and committed. However, unlike their predecessors in the workplace, they will not demonstrate loyalty or stay at organizations for long, particularly if they feel slighted, uncared for, or that their work has little or no meaning to them. Therefore, the value benefits must include enough nuggets that attract them and retain them for as long as possible.

Employees who feel valued, appreciated, and *included*, and are also aligned to the mission and vision of their organizations, are happier, more productive, and engaged. This directly translates to their loyalty and adherence to their organization's brand, products, services and values. These employees know how to deliver the highest quality work products, and it is through this performance that they make the paying customers happy. These attributes of a workplace culture together form the basis and foundation of a Potluck Culture.

I have often been asked by chief executives and other senior leaders about what it truly takes to engage the employee base. Without fail, I have said the organizations that can unleash and leverage the diverse talents, skills, thought leadership, and experience of their people in a culture of inclusion, trust, and openness are the ones that reap commercial rewards. For Millennials—but also for all employees who want to be valued and engaged—this powerful cocktail of leadership know-how is what is expected.

Employees First, Customers Second

While the cornerstone of good business has been the paying customer (along with offering great products and service), what has been sorely missing for most organizations is a focus on *employees first*. This is a call to action for employers to establish authentic relationships with their employees to help them understand what it means to be fully vested in their company. With this, the premise is that *profits follow*.

To strengthen rapport, employees must feel very comfortable with speaking their mind and are in fact encouraged to do so. In such a dialogue-driven work environment, employers who respect this interaction and implement what they learn from the feedback win in their respective marketplaces and industries. Being proactive and timely with appropriate employee-focused actions is the difference needed to keep the company on the right course.

The stakes have never been higher for organizations. The ones who put faith in their employee base and put employee-first attributes in place as part of their operating norms or culture are the ones that are reaping financial and strategic success. This approach, manifested through human capital or talent management programs, enables these organizations to see the fruits of their investment in people. Providing a workplace culture where the employees' developmental needs are addressed proactively is a "must do" for all companies trying to win the battle for talent.

The benefits of focusing on your employees will overflow into building crucial relationships with customers, creating and marketing the next great product or service, and being involved in their communities and environment—all creating the highest level of your employees' engagement.

CHALLENGES FACING THE MODERN WORKPLACE

Therefore, the employer-employee "deal" needs to be revisited and recrafted to engage Millennials and a workplace filled with multiple generations. The deal—also known as the employee value proposition—is the balance of the rewards and benefits that are received by employees in return for their performance at the workplace. In the modern workplace, with multiple generations trying to work in sync, the deal takes on a whole new meaning and design.

A summary of what each generation brings to the table and what perspectives and mindsets each possesses, what influences them, and how they might conduct themselves at work is depicted in the following table.

Table 3. Comparison of the generations[14]

	Traditionalists (1900–1945)	Baby Boomers (1946–1964)	Generation X (1965–1980)	Millennials (1981–2000)
Influences	· Great Depression · New Deal · World War II · Korean War · Tough childhood	· Civil Rights · Sexual Revolution · Cold War/Vietnam · Space travel · Assassinations · American dreamers	· Berlin Wall fell · Watergate · Women's Lib · Energy crisis · Mom works · Single parents	· 9/11 · 2008 recession · Technology · Child-focused world · Digial media · Kept busy as kids
Values	· Hard work · Dedication · Sacrifice · Respect for rules · Duty and honor	· Optimism · Teamwork · Self-gratification · Involvement · Personal growth	· Diversity · Techno literacy · Fun and informality · Self-reliance · Pragmatism	· Confidence · Civic duty · Achievement driven · Respect for diversity · Optimism
Work Views	Prefer conformity over individuality in workplace. Used to strict, vertical lines of authority.	Live to work. Value individuality, creativity and personal fulfillment. Desire to make a difference.	Work to live. Expect work to be fun, and if not fun, better have big rewards.	Insist on work-life balance. Skeptical and unimpressed by authority, more self-reliant. Work is a means to an end.
Feedback Needs	"No news is good news."	"I only need one feedback per year with documentation."	"Sorry to interrupt— how am I doing?"	"I can get feedback at the push of a button."
Work Styles	Can be frustrated by lack of discipline, respect, logic, order, and structure. Respect hierarchy, policy/procedure, and expect people to put needs of others first.	Need to know why their work matters, how it fits into the big picture, and what impacts it will have on whom. Relationship oriented.	OK with direction, but resent intrusive supervision. Prefer regular feedback about work. Will leave job quickly if a better deal comes along.	High expectations of self and employers. Want immediate responsibility and believe they can make important contributions to the company from day one.
Leadership Styles	Hierarchical Directive Controlling	Consensus building Teamwork oriented Participative	Challenge others Inquisitive Competent	Achievers Working leaders Still being determined

The Raging War for Talent

Managing talent in today's work world is challenging. Talent management and succession planning must be developed and executed purposely and with direct alignment to competencies and skills that are most needed for the organization to thrive. Moreover, these skills should be taught, not in classrooms, but as part of the day-to-day job of an employee. Experiential learning has been proven to be the best method to learn skills. In turn, these newly minted leaders will pass on their knowledge to the next level of leaders through a culture of dialogue and feedback. Building a deep succession program is a requirement to succeed in the modern workforce.

So, what is this *war for talent*? The war for talent refers to an increasingly competitive landscape for courting, recruiting, and retaining talented employees. The fundamental powers driving the war for talent include transitions from one age to another—for example, the shift from the Industrial Age to the Information Age or, in today's terms, from the Information Age to the Age of Socially Connected Millennials.

When the war for talent began in the 1980s, economies became more knowledgeable about intellectual capital, and an unprecedented focus on people emerged. As the world's economies continue to become more knowledge based, the differential value of highly talented people continues to mount. We are already in this new world reality, and the war for talent is raging more intensely than ever.

This battle for attracting the best talent has continued also because of the huge demand for high-caliber leadership and managerial talent. Companies need managers and leaders who can respond effectively to the forces of the market, including globalization, deregulation, and technological advances. Moreover, the growing need to retain the very best talent—fueled largely by a new Millennial mindset that constantly desires recognition, feedback, and meaning in work—has made the pursuit for talent even more important.

Today, Millennials account for nearly twenty percent of the US workforce.[15] The sheer volume of Millennials, coupled with the increasing retirement of Baby Boomers, means that employers will be facing leadership gaps. They need to be looking to Millennials to fill this gap.

This leadership fissure is real. Organizations that do not take this seriously by redesigning their leadership development programs and implementing them purposefully, seeking alternative motivational techniques, and nurturing an organizational climate to grow and develop this emerging class of future leaders, will sadly lose the war for talent. When the talent-consulting pundits and analysts present their typical prophetic survey results, they will undoubtedly report that the companies who have done well financially are the ones that have invested in managing, motivating, and developing people—especially Millennials. While all of this is true for the up-and-coming talent, this holds true more than ever before for all employees.

The Conundrum of Social Media

In today's technology-influenced world, social media has opened unprecedented channels of communication and connection. Social media and its vast array of tools and tricks have gained immeasurable popularity across the globe. It is now the easiest way to build relationships in diverse environments. Organizations and their leaders are contending with a new workplace challenge, where people are looking for employers and workplace cultures that value openness and are dialogue driven.

CHALLENGES FACING THE MODERN WORKPLACE

Social media in workplace cultures now clearly impacts hiring and recruiting practices. Communicating inside and outside the company for branding purposes attracts talent. The new target talent group for most organizations is the Millennials, who are most fluent in social media tools. Trying to hire the most talented Millennial is nearly impossible if your company does not have a social media strategy or does not use social media for branding or recruiting. Millennials will jettison from their current jobs to join another employer if the new employer uses social media tools effectively. This raises the stakes even higher in the war for talent.

Moreover, companies that do not use mobile technology through apps—particularly for the younger generation—to manage and develop their careers and schedule their learning portfolios will likely be prone to lose that talent to a competitor. Performance management systems that do not provide texting or instant messaging capabilities will not satisfy the needs of those who seek frequent and regular feedback. Organizations are starting to incorporate social media tools, systems, and techniques to provide instant recognition for exemplary performance, to build a deeper and timelier relationship with their employees.

Even employee health and welfare benefits programs are starting to use social media to recognize, track, and reward employees for maintaining a healthy lifestyle. For example, companies are providing wearable devices (albeit on a volunteer basis) for their employees to track their progress on wellness activities, from how many times they have used the gym to how many steps they have walked each week to maintain fitness.

According to the American Press Institute (API), Millennials rely heavily on social media to get their news, assess the current affairs happening in the world, and, of course, information about jobs and career prospects. API's ground-breaking survey revealed that Millennials use different social networks and all of the popular social media outlets, such as

Facebook, Pinterest, YouTube, Tumblr, Instagram, and Twitter as their conduits for news and information. An amazing statistic from their research is that eighty-eight percent of the surveyed Millennials get news from Facebook at least occasionally, eighty-three percent from YouTube, and fifty percent from Instagram.[16]

I asked one of my Millennial friends, a former student, how she searches for jobs. Amanda, who is currently a job seeker, told me, "Dr. Nair, it's really quite simple. The news comes to me. I have alerts set up on all of the social media sites, and I intentionally follow companies that use them. When a job that I like—one that has my preferences—comes available in those companies, I send in my résumé and biography." She added, "I'm not sure why everyone doesn't look for jobs this way."

Another young professional, Samantha, spent two years in the Bay Area struggling to find a job in the entertainment industry after graduating from the University of San Francisco in 2010 with a bachelor of fine arts degree. She'd always wanted to be an actor. Dismayed and disheartened with the lack of opportunities, her friends advised her to pursue an MBA and told her to take the graduate management admission test (GMAT). However, in a strange twist of fortune, that journey was derailed before she even embarked on it. She saw an advertisement on Pinterest from a tiny start-up firm looking for someone to write blogs. She eventually found something that she could do and enjoy while making a living.

Today, Sam is making about $70,000 annually as the firm's first Internet professional and is taking a couple of online courses on social media content development, as opposed to a fattening her already-large student loans. When I congratulated Sam on her success, she said, "I'm aspiring to be my company's first Chief Marketing Officer."

Social media tools can fortify the employer-employee relationship in ways never imagined previously. The access to a deeper level of communication is indeed contributing to the dawn of workplace humanization, where people are respected and treated as significant resources to achieve the organization's strategic imperatives.

Recommended Strategies for a Successful Work Environment

Organizational leaders, chief executive officers, and other senior management typically focus their energies into building great business or customer strategies. Some may hit the mark and others may not. The ones that didn't hit the mark likely failed to execute the strategy. It is in this execution that today's leaders have an opportunity to bring to the forefront a people-centric culture.

If an environment of inclusion where the good in people, their innate potential, and ability to execute can be cultivated and where employees are well understood and, ultimately, revered, it will include open, transparent, and frequent communication. If honesty, trust, and authenticity thrive, employees will do the necessary things to execute the organization's strategy well. While these strategies may appear idealistic and some naysayers may feel they are too "soft and sensitive" and hard to implement, my experience has led me to strongly believe that, if executed well and authentically, these solutions will have a direct positive impact on a company's bottom and top lines. I also believe that the very notion of employee engagement and getting the best out of people will result in greater and sustained productivity for the company generated by happier employees. To enable such a workplace, five strategies should be implemented:

1. Get the fit right.

Recruiting and hiring practices have evolved from administrative-centered and process-oriented staffing practices to Internet-based, self-service recruiting boards, to the emergence of a strategic function within HR known as *talent acquisition.* Furthermore, social media has raised the stakes even higher. Finding the right talent starts with finding the right candidate with the correct *fit* for the organization. Companies need to hire wisely and purposefully, using the right tools and techniques. It is still critical to identify those who best fit the company's culture.

2. Build a culture of dialogue.

Building a collaborative workplace environment within a culture of mutual respect is now an expectation for all employees—especially Millennials and also for the Boomer. Giving feedback and receiving feedback frequently, while linking the feedback to career and learning opportunities, is a wondrous climate for any organization. It is an absolute must in the modern workplace, which is now proactively demanding it.

3. Take money off the table.

People are smart. They want to know *why* they are paid *what* they are paid. They also want to know how the rewards—especially base salaries—are determined and set. There is nothing to hide. Compensation needs to be demystified finally, once and for all. Doing so takes money off the table and employees (particularly the new class of Millennials) will expect this. They are not purely driven by pay but want to know what's in it for them in return for their hard work and commitment.

One-size-fits-all rewards programs, the likes of which dominate the workplace today, need to be redesigned and repurposed. Nonmonetary rewards need to be included in the definition of rewards and explained to employees thoughtfully and respectfully. Aligning the right motivational vehicles to the appropriate segment is a necessity in the modern workplace.

4. Innovate as a habit.

No company wants to be left behind because they failed to innovate. In today's workplace, there are many opportunities to take advantage of: welcoming markets, lower interest rates, relaxed offshore borders, lower taxes, and deregulation. The stage has never been lit brighter than it is now for companies to innovate. One only needs to peruse the list of the most innovative companies or best companies to work for to see a plethora of new organizations unheard of only a decade ago.

The common factor that these companies recognize is their focus on making innovation a habit—a people-based culture that allows collaboration and creativity. Of the multigenerational workforce, Boomers have stayed around longer than previous generations. At the core of Boomer energy is their experience and managerial savvy. On the opposite side are Millennials who respect authority and genuinely want to learn from their superiors.

The potential of this previously untapped, marriage-made-in-heaven synergy needs to be deeply exploited by leaders and instituted as part of the workplace culture. After all, Boomers have dedicated years of learning and, as such, their brains are programmed for what works now. The time has come to pass on this wealth of knowledge and experience to the up-and-coming workforce. The synergy will undeniably result in a new wave of creativity, innovation and productivity, ripe for the socially connected and digitally wired world. The tech-savvy Millennials are typically idealistic and expect fun and collaboration in the workplace, and they relish this type of relationship.

5. Make work meaningful.

The modern workplace must be redefined. Not doing so has severe consequences, and organizations risk losing the best and brightest talent. More than ever before, today's workers are seeking meaning in their work and expect a lot in this regard from their companies and their leaders. They want to advance in their careers, learn new skills, do more challenging things and be a relevant and recognized part of their company's success. The new generation of leaders expects to participate actively in the selection of their work. They expect their contributions to matter.

While all generations want to be paid well and be competitively compensated, what motivates Millennials is vastly different from other segments. Even though they are the most burdened with debt (largely of the student variety), Millennials are not driven by money or success in quite the manner their parents were. They insist on social principles and want to know what their company stands for and whether they have respect in their communities and marketplaces. They incorporate social responsibilities as part of work, enjoy taking time (during work) to ideate, and also have no inhibitions about working nontraditional hours, coming in later in the day or leaving early from work. They want autonomy, mastery, and purpose in their jobs and expect the same of their supervisors.

A typical "nine to five" workplace mentality and structure will not work for Millennials. They seek flexibility in the structure of the workplace and their jobs. Specifically, they enjoy working on important and complex projects, desire meaningful roles therein and want to be recognized often and publicly for their accomplishments. Organizations should seek to reimagine how work is defined, how jobs are profiled and developed, and how performance is assessed.

Under the auspices of a Potluck Culture, companies and their leaders can do a lot to engage their workforce. As they implement the five essential strategies, companies will enlighten, empower, and fully engage their people to build a winning, high-performing culture.

In Appendix A at the end of this book, I have included an assessment tool to gauge your organization's culture to see how it matches up with the desired levels of a Potluck Culture. Ultimately, though, what it takes to get the best out of your people is prioritizing your organization's commitment and focus on the employees—transcending customers, shareholders, processes, products, services, and productivity.

The Solutions

Chapter 3

STRATEGY #1
GET THE FIT RIGHT

"I am convinced that nothing we do is more important than hiring
and developing people. At the end of the day,
you bet on people, not on strategies."

—Larry Bossidy, retired CEO, Honeywell International

Talent management starts with hiring the *right* employees—those
who will be counted on to help the company build value and delight its customers. In fact, organizations that place deep emphasis on
managing talent strategically and engaging them continuously are the
most successful ones. According to a 2014 survey conducted by the
human capital consulting firm Towers Watson, companies that place
such emphasis on its people are three times more likely to report that
they have highly engaged employees. These same companies, according to the firm, are also 1.5 times as likely to report achieving financial performance and enhancing productivity significantly above their
peer group of companies.[1]

These highly desirable outcomes are accomplished largely as a result of
a holistic, people-first talent approach that places a strategic focus on

talent acquisition or recruiting with a core philosophy of getting the right *fit*. In a Potluck Culture where people are encouraged to bring their best to the table, it is wise to have people around that table who share similar values, have the requisite leadership skills (or want to develop them), and want to be part of a culture that honors them and continually includes them in the quest for business success.

In today's talent management landscape, finding the right talent that is the best cultural fit for your organization can be daunting. It requires insight into how you seek talent, with a keen observation of their personality and work style, and how your organization is perceived on social media. By proactively developing a list of ideal-fit characteristics that go beyond the mere job description, and maximizing opportunities to learn more about candidates through formal and informal interactions (before, during, and after hiring), your company can have greater assurance and confidence in finding the right talent fit.

The Fit

Hiring the right people should be the greatest and
most revered activity for any company.

After all, you are trying to hire the services of people who are entrusted to help your company achieve its strategic objectives. *Finding* talent is a no-brainer, but finding the *best-fit* talent, both in skill set and in culture, is not easy and should not be taken lightly. In the age of Millennials, where not all Millennials have the same skill set or the same career outlook, the notion of fit has become even more important—and equally more challenging. Therefore, organizations that truly value **effective**

talent management place a priority on ensuring a good job fit for all generations of potential employees, not just for Millennials.

In today's multigenerational workplace, one way to maximize job fit is to use talent assessments appropriately in the employee selection process. Talent assessments, or pre-employment screening tests, are used to help employers predict potential candidates' on-the-job performance, their expected longevity with the company and, best of all, their propensity to fit the company's values and culture. Too often, though, these types of assessments are improperly deployed and used as a panacea for talent management. Rather, they should be used as one step in the process of making hiring decisions. This step puts the company in a better position to see what development new hires need to continually experience for the company's cause.

In the modern workplace, where Millennials are expected to engulf the hiring candidate pool, having Baby Boomer and Gen X leaders participate actively and frequently in the recruitment process adds a new dimension to selecting the right Millennials. Good workers are difficult to find, and involving seasoned leaders who have intimate knowledge of the company, its jobs, operations, and its paying customers will help to focus the hiring, not just on stellar individual qualities, but also on the Millennial's ability to fit into the work culture or effectively handle and execute specific jobs.

Blessed are the organizations that have the *right people* in the *right place* at the *right time* for optimal job fit. These organizations operate like high-performance luxury automobiles. Zooming along the highway, leaving lesser ones chugging, sputtering, and eventually dying.

Just as with automobile maintenance, regularly caring for the cultural fit of your employees ensures that you can rely on them to get you to where you want to go.

Finding the right fit means looking at all possible ways to connect with potential high-performing talent. Figure 2 shows several dimensions of that fit. To work, there must be alignment from both the candidate and the company. Each one of these dimensions needs to be addressed throughout the recruiting process, as well as the post-hiring activities, and embedded into the heart of the organization's talent management strategy.

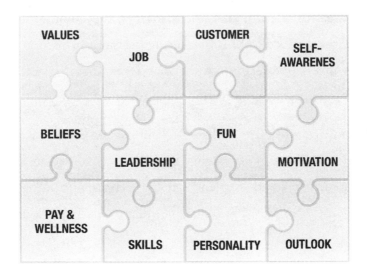

Figure 2. Elements of fit

How to Recruit

The old, tried-and-true recruiting processes and sources of talent will not work well in the modern workplace when searching for the most coveted talent—particularly with Millennials. Millennials, for example, turn immediately to their social media accounts like LinkedIn,

Facebook, Pinterest, Google+, and Twitter to find their dream job. Therefore, companies need to be ready and well-versed to utilize this approach—beyond just being present or visible in these social media circles. According to a PriceWaterhouseCoopers study,[2] nearly half of job seekers (the majority of which are Millennials) use social networking sites daily, establishing social media as one of the most powerful—yet underutilized—talent acquisition tools available to recruiters today.

Making emotional, personal, and individual connections with potential new hires who have a genuine interest in your company's business and industry should be the prime strategy taken by recruiters and HR professionals. Recruiters should want to connect and dialogue with the actual target candidates and view them as their top draft picks (to use a sports analogy). In fact, organizations that do a good job of talent acquisition do this very well. They already have a list of their targeted top candidates and prospects—a sort of wish list with real names and real locations. In other words, they already have a draft pick list.

To further elaborate, consider a talent war room, where key personnel are tasked with finding the best and right fit to fill key positions in their company. This war room may consist of the talent acquisition leader, a business-driven HR professional, the hiring managers for the key positions and other key resources to complete the line-up. The meeting would start with a list of the critical roles or key open positions to fill—each with a summary position description and the critical characteristics and competencies needed for the role. The meeting facilitator would also have gathered and summarized a list of possible draft picks (or ideal candidates) and lined them up against the roles that they would be deemed the best fit for.

Data on these candidates would come from a variety of sources, including internal referrals from trusted employees, prior recruiting knowledge and social media sources, such as LinkedIn. An external recruiter could also be engaged to provide a list of names but not necessarily utilized to manage the actual hiring process. The war room would have a TV monitor with photos, videos, résumé highlights, speaking engagements, education and credentials, publications, and blogs of the potential draft picks. Using this method, companies would be even better prepared to put their best foot forward and identify who they want on their payrolls before the first interview question is asked.

Finding candidates through social channels means asking the candidates to share information via public means. For the process to work, recruiting professionals must be equally willing to share information about the company: its culture, working norms, leaders, and strategic direction. New hires with leadership potential want to work for winners or, at the very least, ones that act as winners do in high-performance cultures. By being this purposeful, companies can enhance the process of getting the right fit early in the process.

When making the sometimes treacherous expedition into social recruiting, sourcers (a new breed of HR professionals whose jobs are solely to source for and locate talent) and recruiters are entering a space in which passive and active job seekers have already shared or collected massive amounts of information on a daily basis. In order to make candidates take note, your company's message and its raison d'être must stand out above all in the unrelenting and crowded cyber traffic.

Presenting job openings in creative ways allows recruiting professionals to showcase the personality, working style, and culture of your organization. Attracting and then retaining those recruits, who are actively seeking out your company because they resonate with your brand, should be the modus operandi for the modern recruiting workforce. After all, both job seeker and company hirers are looking for a good fit.

Millennials, by the way, are the cohort with the greatest propensity for seeking out companies who demonstrate what they say on social media.

Everyone, particularly Millennials, are far more active today on social media and use it for everything, including looking for where they can make a living. Think about it. Don't we find ourselves googling someone the minute after we meet them and, in many cases, before? Therefore, make no mistake—Millennials are already using social media tools to search for and evaluate potential employers. Company recruiting teams should be monitoring and managing their social media presence daily—in particular, sites such as LinkedIn, which is fast becoming the Grand Central Station of job seeking. It is wise to ensure that your company is reflected in the right light.

Using social media techniques and tools for recruiting initiatives requires a focus on substance, not just reviewing résumé details. One other trend to watch for and develop in your own company's recruiting process is video résumés, or video biographies. These are social media-accepted ways to actually see and hear the candidate that may eventually lead your company. Companies must admire candidates who showcase themselves in this manner, tell their story, and portray what they can offer a company.

The process of talent seeking should also start before the future talent graduates from college or a university. The best candidates often have their first job before they graduate and, thus, a smart, social media-savvy company will be successful if it develops relationships with local colleges, universities and the various organizations found within them. Offer job-shadowing opportunities or short-term internships and steward career events on campus to engage with students. While doing so, always find the opportunity to share your story and what matters most to your company.

Finding Fit During the Interview Process

It is possible to hire a candidate who stays and actively contributes as a member of the company and the teams within it. However, most organizations and managers need to dramatically change how they interview and engage employees to hire and *retain* the talent with the core competencies and values that fit the job. They also need to consider what a strong talent looks for in an employer and what the organization has to offer. Starting with the hiring process is the best first step.

The interview process itself needs to be structured, formal, and measurable. Even though Millennials are more laid-back than older generations, they still expect formality and a tone of seriousness in the interview. Millennials then feel they are a vital part of the company's search process.

Discovering the best person to hire (the best fit)—especially with Millennials—is where talent assessments can be quite useful. Its most potent use is to predict future behavior. Millennials may not have an extensive past work experience, but that doesn't mean you can't discover great potential and a great corporate fit. When candidates don't have enough work experience, you have to look for predictable behavior in their life experiences. Even family events can demonstrate how they handle situations—be it stress, confrontation, deadlines, hierarchy, or standing up for their values—whatever is important for the position you are filling.

The key to a behavioral-based talent assessment is that it avoids hypothetical answers and lets you uncover real past behavior, which will give you clear insight into how they will behave in the future. This type of interview also has a side benefit. As the interview progresses, you learn valuable information that helps you build a relationship/partnership and an understanding of their past experiences, stories, and abilities and, most importantly, what development the individuals need.

Within the first interview, hiring managers need to reserve time to discuss their expectations about the job and the expected behaviors needed to thrive in it. Just as importantly, they need to ask Millennials for their expectations, which might include the following questions:

- What are the training, learning, and development opportunities offered by the company?
- What career advancement opportunities and time frames are available?
- How is the salary for the job determined?
- Is there a need to work overtime and will that time be compensated?

A job interview is a *human* event. Even though the stakes are high and recruiting is a serious business that needs to be conducted with formality, it also needs to be friendly and filled with creative experiences for everyone involved. To humanize the process, start by asking the candidates what questions they have. Surely all candidates walk in to interviews with lots of questions on their minds. Your interviews should unfold the way normal human conversations do, where each party takes the time to authentically learn about one another, as opposed to a set of one-sided interrogative querying.

Woven into the interview conversation should be questions centered on why the candidate (particularly the Millennial) is interested in the company, as compared to other organizations, such as the competition, and what exposure to people and work they have that will expand their skill, knowledge, and experience. Millennials are very concerned about the length of the workday and work-life balance. Therefore, part of the dialogue should be about how those will align while working for your company.

Seeking talent in today's labor pool means purposely engaging younger, tech-savvy, creative types who can help a company drive innovation by responding effectively to quickly changing markets, while providing excellent customer service and brand pride. Excite Millennials by demonstrating a winning company and attitude and, primarily, that your company can keep up with them.

If you have a great place to work, then show it. Let them see it as you live out your product and corporate values. It is part of the value proposition of your organization, and there is no better venue to showcase this than the interview process. The results of the well-executed process will illuminate which candidates have the fit right.

Focus More on Quality and Less on Structure

Effective recruiting starts with changing old habits, where too much focus has been on the administrative stuff, like filling out tedious forms, most of which are not technology-enabled. Millennials, for example, crave to be engaged and endeared. They want to feel *wanted*. This engagement, though, must be genuine and must include truisms that resonate with Millennials: a fluid process, a killer app, and dynamic interactions with other Millennials already hired and, of course, with their future bosses. As opposed to filling out forms and adhering to formulaic hiring steps, they relish the opportunity to have meaningful, relevant, one-on-one interactions.

If these interactions are conducted very early in the recruiting process and solid relationships are built during the process, the candidates will feel wanted and get a sense of the type and style of the company that's courting them. Connections through social media outlets enhance this relationship-building phase whereby the company and candidates share snippets of their respective stories. Interactions such as these were never possible in the past, and with the advances in mobile technologies, companies can humanize the recruiting process like never before—all in the name of trying to find the right fit.

All applicants should initially respond to a set of standardized core questions to screen for basic requirements. The flow of questioning can then change according to the applicant's answers; highly sophisticated branching provides an engaging and efficient experience for every candidate. As a result, each applicant also receives a unique interview experience customized on the fly to best suit his or her individual skill set, interests, behaviors and background. This promotes a natural user experience—one that is far more flexible and interactive than the standard static process.

A senior manager I coach, Leticia, had to fill several highly critical jobs in a short time frame as part of her company's plan for expansion to Asia. By her own admission, Leticia had not been as fully engaged as she needed to be in previous hiring activities. In this frenzied recruiting challenge, she sought a diverse group of employees who were self-aware, possessed leadership potential, and were strong self-starters who could be trained quickly and work with minimal supervision—a bad fit in the company's culture, which was based on collaboration and teamwork.

Leticia estimated the types of people needed for her optimal job fit and then began recruiting. She selected applicants based on job applications, résumés, and personal interviews, but she made job offers too quickly. She filled her available positions with good people who did not have the appropriate job and cultural fit. Leticia's speedy hiring process resulted in a poor job fit, which deeply impacted the culture of her company.

The new workers became bored and team performance dwindled. They gossiped, which led to bad feelings. At the end of the day, the employees accomplished little and eventually left the company less than two years later. Leticia's new hires were like mismatched spark plugs, and no one ever checked under the hood. Effective talent management would have included hiring people based on their attributes, as well as the job requirements, to ensure a positive job fit.

Key Questions to Ask

Traditional hiring questions are still critical and a required rubric for hiring in today's recruiting practices. However, the modern take on this is that they should be used more through a conversation rather than presented like an interrogation. If these questions are effectively woven into a respectful dialogue during the interview process, both the candidate and the company representatives can know whether there is a potential fit that can be continually honed and harnessed to help the company achieve its strategic imperatives. The following is a list of traditional hiring questions:

- Does the candidate have the knowledge, skills and abilities necessary for this job?
- What past experiences have prepared the candidate for this job?
- Does the candidate bring strengths that match the requirements for the job?

- Will this candidate be sufficiently challenged in his or her work and in our company?

For Millennials, more organizations now even add another layer of questioning to assess how a candidate fits their culture. Again, when evaluating applicants for your company's cultural fit, hiring managers should also weave these questions into the conversation:

- Is our organization's work meaningful to the candidate?
- Are the candidate's values in harmony with the values of our organization?
- Will the candidate naturally perform and adapt to our culture?

Screening for a cultural fit is an essential part of the selection process, especially for hiring Millennials. There is a greater likelihood that Millennials–even though this is true for all generations today–will stay with an organization where the work feels meaningful and they are introduced, on-boarded and assimilated purposefully into an inclusive environment where they can unleash their potential as quickly as possible. Additionally, when the organization's values are in sync with the employee's values, the employee feels a greater sense of harmony at work which, in turn, drives productivity and retention. That said, never has this been truer than for the Millennial generation–soon to dominate the workplace landscape.

In the modern workplace, the best form or output of talent management is getting the fit right and hiring the right person for the right role at the outset. Engaging the minds and hearts of individuals—before, during, and after the process—can make the end-to-end hiring process one that cannot be undermined.

While I've used and also worked with a myriad of leadership and personal behavioral assessment tools and techniques, the Target Training

International Success Insights (TTI SI) is, by far the most powerful, most accurate and most relevant vehicle for the modern workplace. TTI SI used social and brain science, grounded in tested and proven seminal psychological research, and developed global assessment tools and solutions. These resources have helped hire, promote, retain and identify the best talent in some of the world's best and most progressive companies. Skeptical of tools like these in the past and shunning them for a big part of my career, I've come to realize that not all of them are effective but, in the last few years, I've realized the benefit of such leadership assessment resources and nothing on the market is as impactful and meaningful as those developed by TTI SI. They help people be more self aware, precisely know what motivates them, what jobs they are best suited for and how they can develop and nurture the skills they need to improve on to be effective in the modern workplace. Most importantly, they help build authentic leaders.

Involve the Right Team

Nothing excites new hires, especially Millennials, more than someone from the old guard who takes them seriously and authentically wants them to be a part of their company and participate in its strategic imperatives. Hiring managers from this group, though, need to be ready. When preparing interview notes and questions, these stalwarts need to make sure that the questions are going to help identify particular Millennials with the character traits that not only make sense for the position to be filled, but for the entire organization as a whole. The old guard is the group that has the best background, experience, skills, and knowledge of the entire landscape of the company. Frankly, these are the folks who have the hiring need in the first place. As such, they need to be intensely and actively involved in the hiring process but come into it with a strategy to engage Millennials.

A 2014 study by the ATD (Association for Talent Development) Workforce Development Community, along with Joseph Grenny and David Maxfield, found that potential conflict among generations result in wasted time and lost productivity. In fact, ninety percent of all survey respondents agreed that generational conflict was a time waster and most said they wasted five or more hours of work weekly (twelve percent of the work week) because of chronic, unaddressed conflict among different generations.[3] This is a real issue that organizations and their leaders need to be fully aware of and proactively manage.

Two generations who have the most difficult time working together are Baby Boomers and Millennials. Baby Boomers often see Millennials as lacking discipline and focus. On the other hand, Millennials may see Boomers as having laborious problem-solving skills, responding slowly to the needs and demands of the paying customer base. They also may see Boomers as resistant to change, dogmatic in their thinking, sexist, defensive, and lacking in creativity. The pushback from Boomers is that Millennials are just plain arrogant.

According to the 2014 study, only twenty percent of companies are prepared to deal with this new and daunting workplace reality.[4] These generational conflicts can be minimized, and productivity improved, by communicating to all employees that having an open dialogue about conflicts is expected and is part of the company's culture. Conversations should begin by expressing respect for the other person and the desire to achieve a mutual goal.

The older generations are goal-setting experts, but the twist is to include the Millennials early in the conversation about goals (more on this in the next chapter). These conversations need to be open and honest, describing concerns using facts first and actively seeking the input of the Millennial.

There is an old adage that people leave or join companies because of their managers. People genuinely want to work for bosses who appreciate them. This means success in hiring Millennials is directly correlated to the capabilities and competencies of the companies' leaders.

According to the international consulting firm Deloitte Global, today's Millennials place less value on visible (nineteen percent), well-networked (seventeen percent), and technically skilled (seventeen percent) leaders. In its place, Millennials define true leaders as strategic thinkers (thirty-nine percent), inspirational (thirty-seven percent), personable (thirty-four percent), and visionary (thirty-one percent).[5] Therefore, selecting the right leaders to be active in hiring Millennials is critical. It is vital for companies to assess where their leaders rank on the characteristics sought by today's candidates.

Involve Millennials

High-performing and high-potential Millennials are likely in your company already, with some amazing experiences and ideas to share. This talent should also participate actively in the recruiting process. Not only is this practice valuable in motivating and empowering them, but it also inspires the Millennials you are courting. Seeing other talent like them thriving in the workplace only enhances the chances to captivate and hire them.

With contemporary organizations already getting leaner and flatter, being exposed to Baby Boomer and Gen X senior management is becoming more commonplace for Millennials. Millennials working hand-in-hand with seasoned professionals provides opportunities for them to learn and grow and participate in strategic hiring imperatives, while preparing them for even more impactful leadership roles.

Having Millennials as "influencers" to participate in the interview process also benefits the older generation. With Gen X and Baby Boomers in management positions in the modern workplace, they will benefit from insights into the Millennial mindset and develop continuous innovation, not just in recruiting, but potentially in many other strategic ways.

Millennials also bring fresh ideas and perspectives to the organization, but the success of those ideas depends on finding a great employee-company fit. It would be wise to gain a clear understanding of how the new-hire Millennial likes to give and receive feedback with superiors and colleagues. Ask the new hires to talk about their ideal work-life balance, environmental preferences, how they'd like to be rewarded, and how they primarily communicate. This is not to suggest that companies develop individual customer programs for them but, rather, to get an accurate idea of their next career step.

I often find the "where do you see yourself in five years" question to be a little inauthentic. Most Millennials do not care and are not even close to knowing what they will be doing in the next five years. Alternatively, asking them questions like "After you're hired, how do you plan to advance and grow within our company, and what actions will you take or suggest to continue moving up and gaining experience?" would be a fantastic approach. Millennials want to be a part of something great. If the experienced leaders' demeanor translates that the company can chug along without the input of this new generation of talent, the Millennial will likely move on to another company.

Most Boomers and Gen Xers want to see the world become a better place for their own kids and grandkids. They want to have a direct and tangible way to give back and pass along the things they've learned. There is no better way to accomplish this than to be actively involved in sourcing, interviewing, hiring and onboarding Millennials—and mentoring them. What you get is a match made in heaven and the right prescription for winning business performance.

Engage Millennials Quickly

Millennials are wired for learning.

According to a Pew Research study, more than fifty percent of Millennials say that the opportunity for career progression makes a potential employer an attractive prospect.[6] This is easily the single, biggest motivator for a Millennial: the opportunity to work on challenging work and the true and near-term prospect for career growth.

When asked what makes an employer attractive, one of my former students, Stephanie, a Millennial and a budding social media strategist, told me that she looked for organizations that are "global in the way they think." When I pressed Stephanie to be more specific, she said, "I'm looking for a company that cares about what's going on in the world, has an authentic approach to connecting with people and cultures of all walks, cares about me, and will invest in the time to teach me how to be a global and empathetic thinker." Stephanie went on to say that she does not trust what the websites of these companies state and wants to hear it directly from employees already working there—mostly from the people who interview her.

Further heightening this emerging epic battle for talent is the fact that Millennials will change careers at least once, try a variety of different roles, and will forgo higher pay to find the job satisfaction they seek. Thus, there will be less long-term commitment to organizations. This means that companies will need to be highly committed to a Millennial hiring strategy and an effective onboarding plan that engages them immediately.

The Kenan-Flagler School of Business in the University of North Carolina reported that Millennials, more so than their predecessor generations, appreciate education and learning.[7] Accordingly, Millennials prefer managers who take an educational approach and who take time to understand their personal and professional goals.

A Canadian company that I worked with recently is really on the right track when it comes to hiring for fit and with purpose. Their CEO, Rodney, a lawyer, said this to me:

> Our ability, approach, and intentional strategy is to attract, retain, and manage talent without an overemphasis on compensation, but rather on our company's culture, to create a sense of belonging as soon as our new hires walk into our company. We offer an environment where our employees are cared for, one in which we build long-term relationships and where we wire our people programs to professional development opportunities.

Brevity, Technology, and Fun

The process of onboarding Millennials effectively needs to be technology driven, enabled through mobile applications, and brief in nature, even for the pre-hiring administrative tasks, such as filling out the requisite forms and showing proof of work eligibility. Most of them will likely want to use their own devices once safely in the confines of their new organization. If at all possible, this should be accommodated.

According to Google technologists, ninety percent of multiple mobile device owners switch between forms and screens when asked to complete tasks, using an average of three different combinations every day.[8] They like to "click and learn" and peruse information as they complete administrative tasks.

Giving away gifts in between presentations about ethics or safety policies or while walking through benefits enrollments forms is an effective way to inject fun into the process. Most of all, intertwined with fun and brevity, involving the Boomers and Traditionalists actively throughout the process will put smiles on faces, engage the Millennials effectively and make them really want to work for you.

One of my Boomer peers told me this:

> I love having Millennials, Boomers, and Gen Xers on my team. They fit in perfectly with diversity. It keeps me in touch with what is relevant today and reminds me of the changes my generation brought to the workforce in the 70s. When I see my Boomer co-workers struggling to hang on to "how it used to be" instead of collaborating with others and being excited about the present, I feel they will regret it after they retire.

The older generation leaders can share their stories of what brought them success and how the company became what it is today. Putting these realities and images into the minds of the new hires early in their tenure will bear fruit in the long run. Setting this foundation will give you more involved, actively participating and engaged employees.

Onboarding Revisited

The company's early show of affection needs to continue well beyond the interviewing phase and throughout the tenure of the newly hired Millennial. The best way to do this is to extend the hiring process through the first sixty to ninety days. During this period, the Millennials need to be fully engaged about the job and its duties and the company and its strategic imperatives.

Leaders should be acutely aware of the Millennials' development needs and opportunities to enhance their longevity with the company. Some of this can be gleaned from the talent assessments conducted as discussed earlier. However, the first week of starting in their role to about ninety days into their employment provides the first and best opportunity to truly understand how to best develop this new generation of talent.

In a Potluck Culture, four phases make up the new hire's initial experience. This is the time when the Millennial should be engaged through dialogue and respect and where there is an exchange of knowledge and expectations.

Figure 3. New hire integration

Pre-hire

The hiring process really starts when a potential recruit is being courted by the company. They can be much better at identifying talent if they have a good sense of what type of person they seek, what skills they possess, what their propensity is for continued development (including leadership potential), and whether they fit the culture of the company or can be molded into it. This rubric helps companies find their OKGs. OKG—Our Kind of Guy (Gal)—is a football term made famous by Boise State University. Its recruiting coordinator, Keith Bhonapha, famously once said,

> For us, when it comes to the O-K-G and the type of player that we want, it's not just football. Is he the type of person that we want? Is he the type of student that we want, as well as the athlete? Anybody can turn on film for the most part and say, "Hey, that guy is a good football player." That's easy to do. But when it comes to finding out if a guy will fit to your culture, to your foundation, to the values and morals that you try and build and fester within your program, that's where you have to do the extra digging and the extra research.

It is in that "extra research" that companies can learn from and build a set of standards for the fit they seek. This makes the hiring process much more strategic—finding the right fit means finding the right OKGs with the makeup that will help your company succeed.

In a Potluck Culture, the focus is on the individual. The new hire is connected on social media, where an exchange of dialogue about one another (company and individual) takes place. This intimate "get to know each other" phase is important to establish an early understanding of what the new hire brings to the table and what potential is there to continue to develop him or her. It is also in this phase, via social media and online tools using mobile technology, that most or all of the administrative elements (signatures, forms, tax information, and benefits enrollment) of hiring are handled and concluded. Getting these mundane and routine tasks completed before the first day of work sets the stage perfectly for a rousing and memorable welcome on day one.

Day One

The first day of work is a momentous occasion for the new hires, and a welcome reminiscent of a Hollywood red carpet entrance should be provided. First impressions are vital. New hires know just how important it is to make a good first impression early in their tenure, but it's also important for companies to put their best foot forward gracefully for their newest team members. The candidates wowed the organization and its representatives at the interview. Now, it's time for the organization to wow them with a perfect first day of work.

It's wise to have everything ready before Day One. If new members arrive to find no one is expecting them, or their workspace is not ready, they will feel unappreciated and unwelcome. Pull out all the stops and have a workspace prepared for the new hires with all the relevant tools (business cards, computer, chair that fit ergonomically for health reasons, phone, etc.) ready to go. Assign a teammate who takes them to their new workstation and gives a tour of the office.

In a Potluck Culture, companies are proud to show their new hires that they have a company where the employee is made to feel wanted and cared for. A company tour is vital and a strategic element in a people-driven culture for a new employee's first day of work, even if the office space is small. Most of all, it helps new hires feel comfortable with the new surroundings and helps them get to know your company's culture.

POTLUCK CULTURE

Part of this tour should include introductions to key employees who will assist the new hires in getting integrated as quickly as possible. These resources include their manager, the wellness coordinator, senior executives, teammates, and, if possible, the chief executive. Prescheduled meetings should include a conversation about pay and rewards and how they are determined. It should also include a discussion about nonfinancial elements of rewards, such as learning opportunities, benefits, wellness programs, and opportunities for advancement and building skills.

While it's obvious that new hires will be trained, training for the job and learning the company's key leadership attributes on day one is a must in a Potluck Culture. As such, new hires will feel more confident about their role and contribution to the organization. Training may also include anything from how to use equipment to what is required for specific assignments.

Everyone wants to feel valued and be able to contribute to the company's success right at the get-go. Companies that believe in a Potluck Culture provide their new hires manageable assignments on day one or soon thereafter. This way, new hires can show what they bring to the table early in their introduction. The one thing new employees don't want to be is bored on their first day. It will have them questioning why they are there.

Many new hires may be unsure of the specifics on their tasks or how to get started. It's guaranteed they will have questions during their first few weeks or months at work. Assigning a specific mentor or "buddy" can help them feel more comfortable and confident. Instead of an overwhelming corporation full of strangers, they have one person assigned to help them. Using a simple but tailored new-hire assimilation template will help track progress with whom they should meet and why it is important (see Appendix B, New Leader Assimilation Template and Appendix C, New Employee Assimilation).

In a Potluck Culture, employees are the centerpiece around a belief that feedback is an essential part of the meaning of work. Therefore, at the end of the first day, ask the employees to provide feedback on how the onboarding has worked thus far. Check to see if they have any questions and if there is anything they are worried about.

Asking for feedback will give new employees a chance to tell you what they need for success, making the transition to a new job easier. It will also help you improve your processes wherever you can. Starting a new job is never easy. Many new hires feel overwhelmed, but by utilizing these tips, organizations can make the first day of work a seamless transition and help new employees feel comfortable and welcome.

Week One

By the time new hires have completed the first week of their tenure in the company, they should be comfortable with the logistics of their new surroundings. They should have a draft of the assimilation form completed so they have a compass to guide them through their first sixty days of onboarding. After one week on the job, employees should begin to feel comfortable with their responsibilities, should have met at least one (ideally more) new business contacts each day, should be familiar with their team members (in their department and out) and should be able to walk into your office with any questions. In a Potluck Culture, companies often offer up an informal session of drinks, cake, or something similar with the other team members at the end of week one so the new hires can assess what they've learned, ask any questions to the group, and hang out in a less formal setting.

It is also appropriate to set up a questionnaire for the employees to complete after the first week. Using a five-point scale (one being a minimum explanation and five indicating a thorough explanation), address issues such as their orientation, objectives set, motivation from the manager, assimilation, adaptation, mentor, organizational philosophy, feedback, facility tours, and more. This is a very simple way to address your onboarding policies throughout the process to see when and how progress is made. This is the week where the company should help their new hires feel they are a part of the team.

First Sixty Days

The important thing in the first sixty days is to familiarize the new hires with the company through recruiting and introductions. One shouldn't expect them to make extreme strides from a business perspective during this time, but they should be welcomed as a valued person so they can then dig in. A former HR colleague of mine, Melissa, said to me about onboarding new hires:

> It's important for any employee, but especially for new ones, to be given a combination of smaller and larger projects very soon. You don't want somebody to come in and think only about one big project, so start them off with something a little less intensive to get them started.

This phase of the new hires' tenure is when a company should capitalize on capturing and captivating their hearts. This is a great time to sit down with new hires not only to assess their familiarity with the organization and their role, but also to see how happy they are. You can assess their performance to this point on some of the shorter projects you assigned, while also figuring out where their minds are regarding the bigger picture projects you hired them for. This approach will go a long way in retaining employees.

Asking for more feedback is a surefire way to not only collect ways to improve the onboarding process, but, more importantly, it sends the message to the new hires that their ideas and feelings matter. What did they find the most confusing during their first sixty days? Inquire as to which parts of the processes were most difficult to comprehend and if there is anything that would have helped them get ramped up quicker. Actively gathering feedback is an integral part of an organization that values its people in a profound manner.

The ninety-day mark is when you should start seeing serious results from your new hires. Employees begin to truly feel connected emotionally to their new organization when they start the engagement mindset. Therefore, it is imperative that during this period the company puts its best foot forward to ensure that engagement actually takes shape and materializes.

Ninety days is also the typical amount of time it takes for employees to be fully accepted into an organization (in terms of health coverage, benefits, sick days, etc.). Simply put, by this time they should have a thorough understanding of what will need to be done to advance the cause of the company. Their role in this journey will be lined out through their individual performance plans and goals, which should be in place.

It's essential in a Potluck Culture that companies do their best to make sure new employees are fitting into this culture. They should be included in company meetings, lunches, or other business and nonbusiness outings, as well as any office rituals, such as town hall meetings and CEO all-hands meetings. If new employees don't feel connected within the company, more than likely they will not be motivated to stick around long.

Make the first impressions last through at least the first sixty days by alerting current employees that a new hire is now a new teammate. In a Potluck Culture, anytime an employee sees someone they don't know wandering around the office, they should make an effort to smile and say hello. This simple gesture goes a long way in making new employees (and any other office visitors) feel welcome.

According to the Deloitte study mentioned earlier, less than fify percent of employees believe that their company does a good job of hiring. Even more worrisome is that the survey also showed that only forty percent of employees believe that their company has the mettle and know-how to keep their highly qualified talent.[9] Such unenviable trends are going to persist and worsen as the task of attracting, engaging and retaining up-and-coming talent—Millennials—heightens.

According to the Pew Research Center, this generation of talent is also the most diverse generation ever and will redefine diversity in the workplace. This varied mix of talent includes Hispanic (fourteen percent), African American (fourteen percent), Asian (four percent), mixed race (three percent) and Caucasian (about fifty-nine percent—a record low for this category).[10] Not only does this mean that a one-size-fits-all administrative recruiting process will not work, but the mindsets, upbringing, cultural awareness and propensity for leadership are all variables to be reckoned with for talent managers. It all starts with an appreciation and respect for assessing *fit*.

Chapter 4

STRATEGY #2
BUILD A CULTURE OF DIALOGUE

"The reality today is that we are all interdependent and
have to co-exist on this small planet. Therefore, the only sensible
and intelligent way of resolving differences and clashes of interests,
whether between individuals or nations, is through dialogue."

—His Holiness, the Dalai Lama

You know what? It's absolutely OK to be yourself at work. In fact, being the best *you* is a welcome change in today's workplace. Authenticity, more than ever before, is required and expected in workplaces. Having fun and carrying on respectful conversations with peers, coworkers, and supervisors are fine ways to boost your engagement level and oneness with the organization. These days, letting your hair down, smiling, laughing, and generally being upbeat can't hurt you. It certainly will not undermine your authority but rather boost the connection with your teams.

Engagement levels naturally rise when people treat each other with respect and have meaningful conversations with one another. Therefore, building a culture of dialogue in workplaces—under the umbrella of a Potluck Culture—will augment engagement. Millennials, especially, will not have it any other way and are ready to participate vigorously in such a workplace climate. They will want to stay with a culture where diversity is celebrated, one-of-a-kind experiences are shared, strengths are valued and voices are heard.

At the end of the day, people leave people—not companies. If organizations and their leaders learn to devote their time and energy to develop personal connections with their employees, collaborative teamwork thrives, great ideas are born and new products or services created.

People may leave an organization because of poor managers and the lack of career opportunities. In my experience, it's not because these career opportunities didn't exist within the company, but rather because the leaders and managers didn't communicate those opportunities effectively—formally or informally. They were so busy managing their talent they forgot to build deep relationships with them through high-quality conversations. In other words, they failed to properly coach their best talent—their prized assets of today and tomorrow. The new generation of talent will not tolerate this. Millennials want to learn and expect to advance in their companies at a fast pace.

One of my former C-suite colleagues, Ryann, who was a General Counsel from my Fortune 500 company days, used to tell me, "Every leader needs to have their leadership radars on constantly with absolutely zero tolerance for stereotypes." She went on to say, "If you've taken the time to create a personal relationship with the up-and-coming talent, you'll know what uniquely matters to them and will be able to coach them beyond their perceived potential. They will walk on hot coals for you and will one day take over the company."

What does this mean? Boss less and coach more; talk less and listen more; and ask not what went wrong but what went well and you could make the future successful together. Asking lots of questions—at the appropriate time and only after a healthy dose of listening has occurred—fuels and feeds a rich conversation.

Today, there is an overreliance on HR performance management systems. These tactical, cumbersome, and administrative-focused systems can never be successful unless the processes that underlie them are fueled by a culture of dialogue, feedback, and genuine respect for the growth and development of the employee. Sadly, most organizations do not think this way, and instead place their emphasis on processes and systems. Figure 4 shows the interconnectivity between these three dimensions.

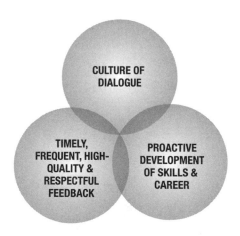

Figure 4. Three dimensions of driving employee
engagement and retention

If executed well and integrated as part of your organization's value system, the result will be fully engaged and high-performing employees all aligned directly with its strategic imperatives. Leaders will receive more valuable and higher quality feedback at all levels of the organization if they value each person, regardless of their position, title, function or generation. Boomers and Gen Xers can lead the charge to drive such a culture of dialogue. For the first time in a generation, a willing audience now exists that yearns to participate in a culture of dialogue—the Millennials.

Rapid-Fire Feedback

Modern workers relish feedback and the more frequent, the better. One way to satisfy the almost insatiable appetite of ambitious and high-potential talent is to help them understand how they're doing through the use of mini-feedback sessions. Providing short bursts of formal feedback on a frequent basis, say, twice a week, can satisfy the thirst for guidance with minimal resources. These shorts bursts can be enabled using testing features on phones. Simple messages, such as "I like what you did at the presentation today. Keep it up," or "Thank you for taking care of that customer. Your influence is making a big difference for us," absolutely help to boost motivation levels—especially with Millennials as well as for rising stars. In fact, such conversations and interactions are the best way to engage, develop and motivate this new generation of leaders. Waiting too long to provide feedback, while trying to gain insight into how much potential they have, can be detrimental.

Timely feedback helps employees make the necessary adjustments to do better and, conversely, waiting too long to provide the feedback disengages them and surprises them if they were not aware of what needed to be changed until it's the end of the year—and too late. No one likes to be surprised. Unfortunately, providing feedback at the year-end culmination of the performance management process is the norm in most companies today. To exacerbate the situation, not only will the employee be surprised if the feedback is given at the end of the performance year, the low performance rating that comes with the feedback is the biggest downer. No one wants to be labeled a number. Those organizations that focus on the conversations and establish a two-way dialogue between employee and manager—throughout the year—are those that get the best out of their employees.

One of my former students, Brian, used to work as an information technology specialist—a very detail-oriented and highly technical job. At twenty-eight, he decided to get an MBA to redirect his career trajectory onto a management track.

Brian had a wonderful personality and was easily the most gregarious and nicest student in my class. He received many compliments from his fellow students about how inviting and collaborative he was. They were the same type of compliments he received from his workplace peers, internal customers and supervisors. As his company expanded, a managerial position became available. He was offered the position, even though he had no management experience. While this was clear to his upper management, they were confident that Brian would pick it up due to his personality, aptitude and attitude. After all, he was about to graduate with a master's degree in business administration. Surely, he must have learned something there!

Brian quickly realized that he had to be resourceful and needed to think on his feet. He learned that his decisions truly mattered and, most of all, his behaviors were noticed—for both good and bad reasons. He began to focus too much on the small things and missed the big, strategic picture. His peers and supervisors thought that Brian was trying to do everything himself so that he would not bother his staff.

Even though Brian was the leader and manager of his group, no one really knew his goals or objectives or where his department was headed. He never enabled his team to showcase their abilities. He did all of the talking and presenting because he thought that was what a leader and manager was supposed to do.

Making matters worse, Brian believed that he had to control and intimidate to get things done, which alienated his own team. His feedback revealed that he sometimes lost his temper, shut down, or was defensive when his ideas were not heard or if anyone criticized him. He did not even think about motivating his team. He thought they should be thankful to have a job and do what their jobs required. In other words, he wanted them to just shut up and do their work.

Meanwhile, Brian's team was beginning to form their own perspectives of their manager. While they valued his technical capabilities and genuinely liked him, they also viewed him as a difficult leader. In situations like this, great companies with leadership that values its talent will identify these negative symptoms fast and incorporate this into their talent management discussions. They form a quick plan of action to remedy the situation, starting with an honest, respectful, and timely conversation with the individual they view as a top talent. In our example, it was Brian.

Once he received the feedback, Brian realized he needed to change his behaviors and actions. Best of all, the feedback he received provided him with a formal performance and development plan to create a clear path forward for promotion and advancement. But, most of all, what makes this story so powerful, is that Brian walked away feeling engaged, wanted, and loved. Companies need to be this resourceful and vigilant when leading and motivating the Millennial generation. What Boomer executives and Gen X managers can do now to play active and willing roles in talent management is simply nonnegotiable.

Brian realized that he needed to take a good look at how he could improve, and this led to an enhanced level of self-awareness and self-management. He thought about people he respected as leaders and realized that they never seemed to get upset and were usually calm. He found that he needed to build trust and make sure everyone saw the same vision for the future playing in their heads.

As Brian met more often with his team (through formal meetings but also more informally during coffee breaks or meals), he asked for their opinions and ideas. He listened like he never had done before, intently wanting to learn from his team. He knew not to let any criticism affect him personally, as everyone wanted to succeed and enjoy their job at the same time. Most importantly, Brian felt that he was a better person overall, and he owed it to his leaders and his company's culture for transforming him. Millennials need to be motivated like this so they don't look for that sense of belonging with your competitor!

From a pure, managerial skills perspective, Brian learned to appreciate the importance of proper multitasking and prioritization. He learned to set agendas and set measurable goals for his team. He linked their goals to his own and, in turn, linked it to the company's strategic imperatives. Most significantly, he communicated this to his team. Brian made the decisions that mattered most in confidence and, in doing so, asked key employees for help or confirmation whenever he was not one hundred percent sure, or when he wanted to expose them to leaders and to leadership settings.

Brian's newfound calmness and self-awareness significantly reduced his stress. He started to act the part of a leader by being more accessible to his team in a self-assured and trusting manner. He had their best interests at heart and tried to motivate by mentoring and coaching to help them grow. He listened to what they had to say and remained quiet until he had something useful or powerful to say. With this new humbled confidence, his leadership abilities improved to where he was promoted to senior manager, was given a major project to lead, and was established on the succession plan in line for a vice president role.

> Companies that introduce an empathetic approach to talent management and succession planning and who truly take the time to assess their leaders for good intentions are the ones that are planting the seeds of future leadership.

These will bear the greatest fruits—motivated, engaged, collaborative, empathetic, and self-aware leaders of the future. These are the future stars who will take companies to greatness and create enthusiastic shareholders.

Stanley, a colleague from my days in financial services, became the VP and head of marketing at a $100 million software development company. As his team was made up mostly of Millennials, he realized he needed to change the way he coached his staff. He spent a great deal of time mentoring—"just talking to" and really getting to know who the stars were and how he could continually motivate them. He said, "My young team wanted constant feedback and information on their career progress."

Accordingly, Stanley instituted formal quarterly reviews and an online, on-demand assessment system that limited feedback to a Twitter-like 140 characters. This approach, with its intended limited words, was far better feedback than a systems-driven process that thrives on year-end feedback. The team, accustomed to instant messaging and texting, loved this. The frequency of the feedback bursts, the brevity of the advice and the encouraging suggestions for improvement felt digestible and timely to them. "What was even more powerful," continued Stanley, "was that we were not slaves to the standard HR performance management systems, but this new culture of feedback also allowed my rising stars to hear quickly from a broad set of people and find out whether they were on the right track."

Instead of waiting for a full-blown feedback process that took weeks to compile, was hard to digest, and filled with mostly negative feedback, as a leader, Stanley would invite every employee to send requests for feedback to five (or more) people and ask, "How am I doing? Was the information relevant? What can I improve and did it cover the content you needed?"

For the Millennials, this rapid-fire feedback mechanism, fueled by mobile handheld instruments (cell phone or tablet), forced them to think carefully about their responses. Because they had to respond immediately, they were able to receive useful detail. For the HR team, this also proved useful as the software involved also collated the responses into a performance dashboard, so employees could track their own private trend lines on skills they were working to improve. The portfolio-like report could be used proactively by all parties to benefit the team and organizational outcomes.

Take the Fear Out of Performance Evaluations

High performers in an organization recognize that the performance management process recognizes and rewards their hard work, performance and potential. However, performance management is typically viewed as a necessary evil, a one-sided affair (usually favoring the evaluator) where fear and uncertainty are ever-present. Taking this fear out of the performance evaluation process is a *must*. The best way to do so is to focus on regular, high-quality conversations between the leader and the employee.

Experienced leaders have the organizational know-how to be phenomenal mentors to the rising young leadership. Leaders demonstrate brilliance as they drive the right dialogues. In today's diverse workforce, with multiple generations working together, there is an opportunity to enable and promote such conversations. Millennials expect and anticipate them but still may grow to fear them if they are not conducted well.

Here are five recommendations to take the fear out of performance management and be authentic when trying to understand and evaluate your direct reports:

1. Let your employees lead.

Employees should view the process as their own and know that the managers or leaders are there to facilitate this in a *forward-looking* manner. The outcomes of the process are a joint effort and both managers and employees can share in that future success.

2. Set goals early.

Using the S-M-A-R-T (specific, measurable, action-oriented, realistic, and timely) tool to develop meaningful goals early in the process is a *SMART* move (see Appendix D in back of book). Goal setting should be conducted as part of a *conversation* where the employees are empowered to draft their goals upfront. During the conversation, both parties can make adjustments as necessary so that they are aligned and the goals are rooted in exceptional outcomes.

3. Enhance quality of conversations.

Performance conversations should be more about the *developmental* needs of the employee (and also of the reviewer) rather than on what was done wrong. A good way to enhance the quality of the conversations is to start them with a positive note and include respect and empathy.

4. Ensure frequency of interactions.

Performance assessments should be done as frequently as possible so that performance is on track to attain the aspired common goals. Frequency levels can vary and there is no golden rule for how many instances of feedback are needed. However, a rule of thumb is for companies with a people-focused Potluck Culture to employ daily feedback and schedule at least three formal sessions throughout the performance year. The daily interactions can be conducted in as little as a two-minute conversation, just to give the employees a sense of reassurance that their managers are there for them. The key is not to surprise the employees at the end of the year with critical feedback they may not have been aware of earlier.

5. Make it collaborative.

Performance evaluations should be informal and conversational. This enables both the leader and employee to build shared understanding and enhance intended outcomes. A collaborative approach takes away the fear that most employees have of performance management. It encourages each party to learn about one another, so that they both walk away from the process with opportunities to continue developing.

In a people-first organization, leaders demonstrate true authenticity. They focus on conversations, take the fear out of performance management, and don't focus on rating scales or label people with numbers. This philosophy builds the commitment that fuels a winning, high-performing culture.

Being the Best You That You Can Be

Baby Boomers and Gen Xers have, over the years, built great foundations in the general management of organizations. However, they both were and still are driven by adages, such as "living to work" or "working to live" philosophies, respectively. They may not appreciate a middle-ground philosophy that places a deep focus on the people who make up their organization.

Organizations that tap into purposely articulating, nurturing and, ultimately, integrating a culture of dialogue will leave their competition in the dust. The need has never been greater for companies to fill the growing leadership deficit through succession planning and the development of emerging leaders to take the organizational mantle forward.

A leadership *reset* is needed in today's organizations, as employees want their managers and leaders to be easy to work with and likeable. They are looking for potential role models who understand their needs and can authentically motivate and energize them in a workplace culture designed to deliver the best results for the organization.

STRATEGY #2 BUILD A CULTURE OF DIALOGUE

Being the best you that you can be requires work and focus. It means taking a genuine interest in bettering yourself and also being authentic in what you do and say. It also means showing a genuine interest in others and helping to make them better. A former CEO I used to work for once said to me:

> People know when you're truly interested in them. If you're not showing a genuine interest—asking thoughtful questions and reflecting upon their answers—your interaction can actually have an opposite effect to the one intended. Take care to remember names, dates, and important life events about them. Don't do it because you have to but because you *want* to. That's being authentic.

Thinking before acting or speaking is a critical people skill that comes directly from learning, listening to others and observing the world around you. The same CEO would say to his leadership team, "Listen to your teams with good intentions. They rely on your leadership. Be trustworthy because it allows you to wisely select friends and associates, determine reactions and responses, and make sound decisions." Another C-suite executive I know well, who now leads the HR function for a massive international bank in Asia had this to add to this discussion: "Pay attention to your gut, Ranjit. It often has something valuable and truthful to say to you."

There's a good chance that at some point in your career, you'll have to sell others on your ideas, products, or services. Whether you are a manager, up for a promotion, pitching a cool idea for a customer, or selling raffle tickets, you need to be able to form a strong, convincing argument for why your idea, product, or approach is worth considering.

Being known as someone who keeps an open mind also makes you more approachable and easier to work with. Only in a company that truly cares about its people (such as in those that fly the flag of a Potluck Culture) can we see these types of skills being revered and used as strategic elements for the company to succeed.

Understanding Developmental Needs

It's important for older leaders and managers to be savvy about their direct reports' strengths and weaknesses. They should also strive to give just-in-time feedback when they notice something not quite right. Sometimes, up-and-coming leaders (especially the Millennial generation), will plunge into specific jobs or careers without truly knowing what those jobs are really like.

For example, some budding leaders will try a hand at sales management, which requires, among other things, the gift of gab and a customer-centric approach to work. However, just because they are great salespeople doesn't mean they will be effective leaders. Therefore, it is important to provide this feedback immediately upon seeing the issue or behavior. A great salesperson might attain or surpass all sales goals in his or her sales performance or incentive plan, but if the individual does so in unethical ways, or disparages others in the process, then that behavior needs to be stopped immediately. But because there is real talent there, companies that honor *people* under a Potluck Culture will recognize the need to develop that individual and help him or her build better self-awareness and the appropriate leadership skills.

The Traditionalist leader, for example, still typically employs old school ways of doing things that make it difficult to engage a workforce that is more diverse and multigenerational than ever before. Today's short-term, rapid-pace, limited-resource workplace requires more trust among employees, transparency in communication and require-ments, and cross-functional collaboration to fuel desired outcomes. Employees want to know quickly what they need to do to succeed and how they should behave to win. They seek an awakened, dynamic spirit to come alive at work. This spirit can be awoken through bril-liant workplace dialogue and a culture of feedback.

Most people—especially those who are high-performing—want to learn and, more importantly, want their leaders to constantly develop them. Under a Potluck Culture, this is a natural occurrence—feed-back, development needs; feedback, development needs; feedback, development needs.

Eliminate "HR Speak"

Remember my inauspicious career entry into the world of HR? The new generation of emerging leaders doesn't want an "HR story," or "HR speak." As a former head of HR, it may be blasphemous for me to say this, but most HR professionals are notorious for using terms that most people just don't use or understand well enough—euphemisms. These are terms such as inclusion (instead of diversity), rightsizing or downsizing (instead of telling the truth that one is being fired), learning organization (as opposed to teaching employees skills to better themselves), and performance improvement plan (a planned way to exit someone from the company).

Instead, people want to hear directly, straightforwardly, and candidly from their leaders on what the definition of success looks like at their company. They are tired of excuses and just want people to be real about how they feel and honest about what needs to be accomplished.

POTLUCK CULTURE

Employees are fed up with office politics and the corporate rat race and are ready to start having fun again. They want a workplace that is challenging, encourages trial and error, and makes them feel that they matter.

I was at an executive roundtable discussion on emerging workplace trends where a fellow panel member—a finance executive whom I'll call Patricia—was asked to share a few words about her leadership experience with the organization. At first, she said all of the "right" things (HR speak), but then she decided to come clean and threw out a bombshell.

She put the whole room on the edge of their seats by expressing dissatisfaction with her own lack of leadership and empathy. She went on to say that even though she knew people were unhappy with her organization's leadership policies, structure, and culture, she regretted not speaking up or doing anything about it. Her poignant words still ring in my ears: "I am a leader in this company and I cannot outsource the leading and managing of people to the HR function. I—no one else—must do it and do it well and with deep conviction and a genuine interest in helping others be better. It is my duty as a leader and my responsibility to my team."

Patricia concluded by talking about "courageous leadership" and why the workplace demands it now more than ever before. She tearfully vowed to start mentoring the up-and-coming talent at her organization and to volunteer as a steering committee member on talent management and succession issues in partnership with her company's HR leadership team.

There were a couple of lessons I learned and took away from this experience. First, everyone has a responsibility to make others better in their organization. Helping others succeed is not the role of just one function—namely HR. Rather, it is the responsibility of all leaders and managers in the company to manage talent, spot development needs, identify their own successors for their roles, and give people a chance to learn new skills. In other words, it is everyone's job to get the best out of people.

Second, no matter how frustrated, troubled, or dispirited someone appears on the surface, deep down, everyone I have met and worked with is truly extraordinary. Yes, there are, of course, those who just don't fit your company's culture, are disruptive, or just are not coachable. The important thing in these cases is to recognize this early and then respectfully try and change them or gracefully exit them from the company. These situations should be few and far between in a Potluck Culture where people are revered and continually engaged and developed.

However hidden, the jewels of goodness, will, and potential in the human spirit are always there—in you, in me, in those we coach, and in those we are helping develop. Perhaps now, we can come to know and appreciate more fully our capacity for the endurance of people, their innate capabilities, untapped potential and the brightness of our human spirit. In a Potluck Culture, this reverence for people is built in all leaders and managers because they believe that, given an opportunity, people will rise to the challenge and bring their best to the table.

Pass Down Information Quickly

Being a phenomenal communicator is a core leadership competency, a critical skill that leaders must have to build winning companies. Courageous leaders fuel their desire to earn trust and respect with a culture of dialogue. Being a great communicator also means holding no secrets, passing on critical information timely and not being afraid to share the source of that information, its meaning and impact on the company and its people.

For example, if there is a piece of news that might impact the company—say the acquisition of a new customer or the resignation of a key leader—unless the information is truly confidential, leaders and managers should share it and explain its significance or consequence with their employees well before they hear it through the grapevine or an all-employee communiqué. No one wants to be surprised. No secrets should be allowed unless they are critically confidential.

Moreover, never stop communicating your company's vision, goals and objectives. Be a great communicator who uses all available methods to define your expectations and set the tone for your company, department or function. Avoid being vague because you will run the risk of losing trust from others.

When I was in the C-suite, I often held informal (at times impromptu) employee or town hall forums. The goal was not to deliver a "state of the company" address or some other important announcement; it was to address questions directly from employees. The objective was to communicate the truth about how the company was doing, how we were viewed in the marketplace and what we were doing to beat the competition and win. We recognized people simply wanted to know what was going on, and these opportunities afforded the chance to teach and coach employees as well.

With the modern workplace's unprecedented diversity, the opportunity for the older generation of leaders to mentor the up-and-comers has never been more prevalent. The workplace has become both more delicate and more demanding, and employees want to know what behaviors and results they are being held accountable for and what they can or cannot do. Experienced senior leaders are often very structured about how they communicate. However, it is quite noble to just be human and approachable to your teams, especially to those you feel have the potential to take over the reins for you in the future.

With such a culture, leaders can also build a culture of gatherings where vital information can be passed on in a timely manner. These forums help identify the real leaders and cheerleaders. Just as importantly, you will discover those who need help and which ones may put up roadblocks. Great communication can be spawned in a culture of dialogue and can be vitally effective where accountability is valued.

Dialogue is a form of conversation where people genuinely try to assess different mindsets, ideologies and perspectives to enable a new understanding. In an organization where dialogue is practiced, the likelihood of building a people-centric culture is enhanced tremendously. The culture seeks to discover a new meaning that was not previously held by any of the participants (managers, leaders, or employees) in the dialogue.

In a Potluck Culture, all employees should be able to learn from one another and help get the best out of each other. To do so effectively requires an innate ability to converse and interact well. These skills can be practiced and need to be included in today's workplace, where rising stars, such as Millennials, expect them of their managers and leaders.

While quite difficult to achieve, specific skills can be honed to build such a powerful culture (see Figure 5).

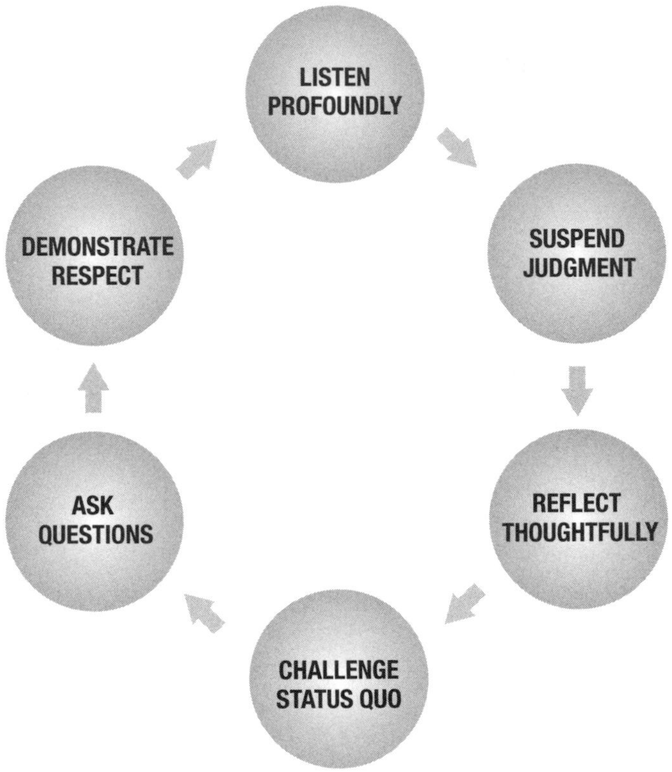

Figure 5. Being awesome at dialogue

Listen Profoundly

In its most simple form, profound listening involves gradually silencing bias-infusing voices in our heads so that we can hear the true story a person is telling. As we listen to appreciate and understand their holistic story, we remain silent, suppressing the natural desire to interject, and merely listen.

One leader I hold in very high regard, a CEO and one who has mentored me in the past, used to tell me, "I'm amazed at how much I really take in about people and their ideas when all I have to do is listen to them." This leader successfully focused on understanding the speaker instead of being prepared mentally to interrupt and offer an opinion or idea.

Deep listening can occur anywhere, anytime. It could be with a teammate, a superior, a customer, or someone trying to sell you a product or service. The common factor in all these interactions is the genuine choice to listen. It is both powerful and important within a Potluck Culture.

Demonstrate Respect for Others

Voltaire, a French author, humanist, rationalist, and satirist is reported to have said, "I do not agree with what you have to say, but I'll defend to the death your right to say it."[1] This perspective lies at the heart of respecting others. This is particularly difficult to do when we interact with people who have contrasting views to our own.

While respecting others does not mean that you have to agree with them, it does mean that you will allow them the time and space to have their say. Their perspective is valid in the context that it contributes (even if only in a small way) to understanding the complete picture they want to communicate.

Ask Probing Questions Without Intrusion and Balance with Advocacy

Open questions enhance the understanding of different perspectives or allow the deeply held mental models that lie behind many perspectives to come to the surface. Voicing openly is the capacity to say what you think *and* to be able to explain why you think as you do. All views are important for the development of a true understanding of a situation.

Unfortunately, many people struggle to share their views. If those views are not shared, then a part of the picture is missing. Balance sharing your views by asking genuine questions to better understand another person's view, or allow the group to talk about issues that will enhance the whole group's collective understanding of a topic. Practicing this skill significantly enhances the quality of your contribution to the conversation.

Challenge the Status Quo Openly Without Arrogance

In a Potluck Culture, all employees are considered leaders in their own right for what they bring to the table. It is entirely appropriate to give them permission to question the status quo of their organization.

Status quo thinking may have developed due to time or prioritization constraints, or the culture may have a "if it's not broke, don't fix it" mentality. The issue, though, is that companies and their cultures are living and breathing entities that change with the people who inhabit them. In a Potluck Culture, exploring new ways of doing things is healthy for the organization and also for the people who shape it.

Companies that honor people and place their intellect first enable and invite *all* differing perspectives. As a leader of such an organization, you may think that certain training practices or policies are working because no one is saying differently. Have you ever really asked, though? Invite differing perspectives from within your organization to examine issues, and be thoughtful about whose perspective can really lend a fresh point of view. The goal should be to get the people who are affected by specific policies and training to the table for the discussion.

One of my previous managers challenged me once to start asking more questions. I asked him why this was important. He said,

> When a fellow employee comes to you and has an issue with the current status quo, take this opportunity to get curious with them and ask questions about why it's not working and what they would do to fix it. Maybe a major overhaul isn't even in order, and it's a simple adjustment that can make everyone more engaged. These one-on-one opportunities with your team are great ways to, little by little, shift away from the current state of affairs towards something more meaningful. Most of all, you look like someone who cares about the company when you ask questions. There is a sense of genuineness and authenticity that asking questions demonstrates.

Suspend Assumptions and Judgments

The capacity to explain why you hold certain views lies at the heart of suspending assumptions and judgments. Much like hanging clothes on a line to dry, suspending means presenting your views and opinions for others to consider. This allows people to look at them, question them, and assist you in developing a deeper understanding of your perspectives.

To suspend your assumptions and judgments illustrates a willingness to be vulnerable, which is a key attribute of a servant leader. Should you discover that your views are not useful, you have the opportunity to adopt new ones. This experience is often described as true learning.

Potluck Cultures are filled with servant leaders, those who value diverse opinions and genuinely appreciate the ideas and contributions of others. These leaders value what everyone brings to the table in their organizations. Under a Potluck Culture these leaders do the following three things regularly and are known for doing so:

1. Cultivate a culture of trust.

In a Potluck Culture, employees don't congregate at the water cooler to gossip. "Yes" people or those practicing pocket vetoes are rejected but coached to stop those behaviors. I'm sure I'm not alone in observing meetings where everyone is nodding and agreeing with a decision, and at the end of the meeting, it looks like the course or decision is set. But it isn't. As soon as the meeting is over, someone sarcastically comments, "That's never going to happen." Outside the meeting room, the participants cluster like sheep, saying that was a ridiculous meeting or remarking, "We'd never support *that*." Instead of taking action, nothing is done and the company's culture is drastically injured.

2. Develop other leaders.

Leaders leading other leaders through experiential, on-the-job learning is part and parcel of a Potluck Culture. The repeatability factor is critically important. It means teaching others to lead, providing opportunities for growth and demonstrating by example—all done as part of the job and encouraged by the culture of the company and its leaders.

3. Encourage others.

The trademark of a servant leader is motivating and encouraging others. One of my previous bosses, John, did it best. When introducing others, particularly younger rising stars, he made it a habit to describe them to others as important and critical teammates. He would say, "Let me introduce you to Ranjit. He is one of our future leaders. You're going to like working with him. He is talented in many areas, and I'd encourage you to meet with him and get to know him." Being introduced like that only humbled me, while making me feel ten feet tall. A true servant leader says, "*Let's* go do it," not "*You* go do it."

Reflect Thoughtfully

Our fast-paced world offers little time to reflect. However, reflection enhances your communication skills and capacity to dialogue through considering how you have just practiced your skills. In team environments, it is worth holding a reflection at the end of a conversation to recognize where the skills of dialogue were used effectively and where they could be improved.

Finally, in a Potluck Culture, always be ready to help enable change. If you don't want to change a policy or training because it's working or perhaps to change it is unrealistic at this time, communicate this to your team. Don't waste everyone's energy getting feedback if you're not going to do anything with the information. There is no quicker way to lower your emotional capital as a leader than to ask for new ideas and then ignore the input. Not only are you setting a false expectation, it might send the message that their ideas aren't good enough. Both have much worse outcomes than sticking with the current process or policy.

Summary

People often recognize that practicing dialogue or conversation is not easy. It really and truly isn't. However, the learning process is driven by conversation. Practicing these skills will provide immense benefits for improved personal and team performance. Conversations will help shape direction, as employees engage with one another and, more importantly, with the management team.

Sociologists have labeled such a dynamic exchange of thought, ideas, and expressions as conversation theory. Conversation theory addresses the way learning takes place and the creation of an appropriate learning environment. The idea is that real learning takes place only through meaningful conversation. The learning generated is what drives knowledge and, accordingly, action and change. Not all learning must take place in the form of a conversation, but for real learning to occur, a deep, inner, and essential conversation must take place.

Dr. Simon Fletcher, a colleague of mine from the United Kingdom, told me, "If the teacher is able to learn from a discussion of the subject matter, the discussion becomes more tangible, more practical or real, and most importantly, more relevant for all those involved in the conversation." The inference is that in a Potluck Culture, all employees in the setting have a say in the outcomes of an event or in the success of the enterprise.

A ladder effect emerges in which each contribution has the ability to move all the participants up the ladder of comprehension and aligned responsibilities. Equally compelling is the concept that the exchange and dissemination of ideas and understanding of objectives should be on an equal level, which means the conversation should take place without hierarchical structures or top-down directives. In the executive setting, this is important because the management of the people process is an entrusted role that all employees need to be invited to participate in. With diverse minds getting together in a Potluck Culture, each employee becomes a teacher or a provider of knowledge, transforming the organization into a community of learning.

Chapter 5

STRATEGY #3
TAKE MONEY OFF THE TABLE

"If you pick the right people and give them the opportunity to spread their wings—and put compensation as a carrier behind it— you almost don't have to manage them."

—Jack Welch, retired CEO, General Electric

All employees—at their core—are ambitious and eager to do their jobs well, and they want their careers to get off to a flying start as early as possible in their employment. While this is especially true for the Millennial generation, it is also true for all well-intentioned employees. When describing their ideal jobs, today's employees are more likely to value opportunities for career advancement and the chance to learn new skills than previous generations. They also value nonmonetary compensation, such as the ability to work from home and flexible schedules—benefits that reach beyond the paycheck to improve the quality of their lives.

A 2014 survey conducted by Towers Watson[1] revealed that the top three motivators for employees from all generations are money, career and learning. If this is true, then there is an opportunity to *take money off the table* and demystify pay once and for all. Then managers and leaders can spend the necessary and much-needed time to develop the requisite skills of their employees.

Total Rewards

In virtually all cases, the more people know about how they are being compensated, the better they feel about their pay and benefits. The first thing to get straight is the definition of what is now called *total rewards* in the modern workplace. Total rewards are about more than just the number on a paycheck. Total rewards include all of the ways in which the organization compensates employees and supports them and their careers, starting with the following six:

1. Benefits.

Traditional examples include health insurance, vacation, retirement plans, and life insurance. Most employers do not discuss benefits until they are ready to extend an offer. Why is this the case? Benefits cost companies a lot of money, but too often they are not discussed in detail or given enough credence. Even then, companies typically just send information to the prospective employees about the benefits package, essentially relying on them to determine the value of those benefits.

Don't leave it up to the prospective employee to figure it all out. Sit down and have a conversation about benefits. Not everyone has the same benefits needs and a one-size-fit-all does not bode well in the modern workplace. Create the opportunity for questions and explanations.

2. Work-Life Balance.

A company with a strong work-life philosophy supports efforts to help employees achieve not only success but also improved health and quality of life, both within and outside the workplace. Onsite wellness centers, concierge programs, and employee support programs fall under this category.

Work-life balance is a bit of a misnomer in today's vernacular. It used to mean that people were given leeway to work from home or attend to personal needs during work hours. That was, in essence the definition of work-life balance. However, in this modern workplace, where the line between work and life is either somewhat blurred or nonexistent, companies employing a Potluck Culture absolutely trust their employees and do not restrict or place unnecessary expectations on them to be present at work during so-called "normal" office hours. In such cultures, there is the freedom to work on special projects and choose what to work on and when to work on them.

So long as the expected deadlines and deliverables are met, managers operating in a Potluck Culture provide their employees the chance to have autonomy to work independently. They trust their employees to do the right thing, and frankly, that's what employees expect in the modern workplace.

3. Performance and Recognition.

This includes how employees are acknowledged and rewarded for their efforts and achievements at work. Having a performance management process that has its foundation built on regular, high-quality, meaningful feedback and fueled by a culture of conversations and dialogue is, in itself, a reward of work. Employees relish such an environment where they are taught and nurtured to do the right thing and learn the right behaviors under the auspices of a Potluck Culture.

In addition, employees want to be recognized—timely, I might add—for their accomplishments. These recognitions will be even more powerful if done well and communicated broadly so that all employees see who is accredited and for what. Potluck Cultures honor people and revere them through timely recognitions, whether they are accompanied by monetary rewards or not. In many instances, a simple handwritten note or a few powerful words of gratitude at the start of a meeting go a long way to engage the recipient. These are examples of rewards with no money at stake.

4. Development and Career Opportunities.

Growth opportunities, training and other learning experiences help employees pursue their career goals. Employees expect this and see these opportunities as rewards—nonfinancial rewards. They want you to believe in them and invest in them. Rewards such as these are a mainstay in Potluck Cultures, and they come at very little cost to the employer. Giving someone a chance to learn a new skill on a special short-term project is an example of such an opportunity.

5. Compensation.

This is the paycheck. Employees may have fixed pay (base salary) plus variable pay (commission, bonuses, stock, etc.). Under a Potluck Culture, money is taken off the table. Of course, that does not mean that pay is low or below market, but it does mean that all elements of pay are explained well.

Base salary, for example, is a fixed element of pay, and there is a level of science behind how it is determined for a job and the individual who is in it. While the basis of this determination is largely driven by the market for such a job and the organization's position in that market, suffice it to say that explaining how it is determined is the best and most basic thing that managers can do for their employees. The most effective reward programs are not the most elegantly designed but those that are communicated and deployed most effectively. In a Potluck Culture, all managers have no qualms about explaining all elements of pay to their employees.

6. Emphasize Nonfinancial Rewards.

Employers who do not emphasize and communicate nonfinancial rewards when bringing in employees are missing out on a key opportunity to differentiate themselves. Potluck Cultures honor this emphasis and look forward to these discussions and conversations about pay and performance. For example, when making a job offer, focus on all elements of pay (including all benefits) and not just the base salary.

When I was the head of HR for a large global company, Tim, the head of Compensation and Benefits (Total Reward is what we called the role) said this to me, "I think it is a travesty and a huge, missed opportunity," he said. "You do not want to talk about it too soon, but benefits are worth some additional communication instead of just calling and saying, 'here is your $80,000 salary offer.'" When this happens, people tend to only hone in on the salary number instead of looking at the full range of rewards a company offers, such as variable incentive pay, spot bonus recognition opportunities, paid time off, a foreign assignment, or other learning opportunities. "We have a total rewards concept and philosophy. We offer much more for the hard work of our employees rather than just base salary. So, we should focus on the bigger picture," he lamented.

Even though no organization can or should make promises regarding career advancement to an individual, the organization can provide examples of those who have prospered with the company. Similarly, companies can sell training and development opportunities as a signal of the organization's willingness to invest in their employees. This makes all the difference for people, especially when you really want to hire them because they're your first-round draft picks, and they may be considering multiple offers.

In today's typical organization, most of the categories of total rewards are fairly standard throughout the organization, with the exception of compensation.

Determining Compensation

When determining compensation for employees, organizations typically consider the following four aspects:

1. Internal Equity.

What are other people in a similar job or with similar experience within the company making?

2. Market Pay.

What are other companies paying for similar jobs? Companies obtain this data by purchasing salary surveys.

3. Qualifications, Credentials, and Certifications.

Why and how is the employee qualified for this job? More relevant experience or more relevant education will often result in higher pay.

4. The Total Rewards Philosophy of the Company.

This varies by company and can change as the company changes. For example, start-ups typically have a philosophy of paying lower on base salary but offering stock that will be worth more if the company docs well. The philosophy on pay for a particular company is also based on its affordability, the company's position in the market compared to its competitors, the company's own stage in its life cycle, and its say on the mix of pay. The latter merely means that the company may focus on fixed elements of pay more than variable elements of pay, or vice versa.

What's most important is for employees to look at the bigger picture. Is the company being truthful and open about its pay practices? Does it honor the intelligence of its people? These factors play off of one another. For example, you may find a company with really great pay and benefits but is lacking in learning opportunities, offering challenging work, flexible schedules and performance and recognition. Pay alone won't keep the best talent if they can find a better balance and greater opportunities elsewhere.

> **Compensation is still a deep, dark secret and mystifying for most employees. It doesn't have to be that way. It is way better for companies to be upfront and honest with employees about it.**

After all, people will go to Internet sources to figure out whether they are paid commensurately for what they have been asked to do.

However, doing this may give false data and inaccurate assessments of pay levels. Every company is different and pay levels depend on a whole host of factors.

Demystifying Pay

Money is naturally a "must have" and a conversation about money is a "have to have." People want to be compensated fairly and, indeed, competitively, so that they feel they have been taken seriously and paid proportionately to their skills and their levels of contribution to the company. Most of all, they want to feel that they have not been cheated out of what's fair. Even though they must make money to pay the bills, research has shown that money only motivates people to a certain point. Once money is off the table, this is when the real, people-centric culture shift can take place.

While people leave companies and jobs largely because their managers have not engaged them, or they simply do not like their jobs, pay is still at the top for reasons why people stay at a company. However, the fallacy is believing that people stay to get greater pay. This is just not the case, and it is particularly not the case for Millennials. People (especially the younger generation) want to know *why* they are paid *what* they are paid for *what* they have been asked to do. They want to know the details of how the pay was determined, particularly their base salary.

Base salaries are naturally hierarchical; the more importance you have in the company or the greater impact your skills help the company, the greater your salary is. That said, I don't believe any company should ever ask what someone's previous salary history was. That's really not the company's business. When I make an offer to new hires, I always ask them what kind of salary they're looking for and how much would be enough to get money off their minds. There's no issue in asking about salary in this manner.

When the salary question is presented in the right way, I find most people are honest about their needs. However, the issue is that most people don't have a clue as to how salaries are determined in the first place! While the scope of this book is not about the mechanics of pay and how it is set up, I can tell you that the process is generally very straightforward and explainable. Leaders just need to honor the intelligence of their employees and tell them the truth. People are generally very astute and, if you explain it correctly, they will "get it." This way, people will not be distrustful and any questions about whether they are paid appropriately can be taken off the table. The focus can then be shifted to how their company is going to develop them.

Offering Things Money Can't Buy

Once the money issue has been laid to rest, you can focus on offering a work environment that truly makes people happy, both in their personal lives and their professional lives. You want them to feel that they have opportunities, no matter what direction they want to go. You also want them to know that the organization is willing to make changes at their suggestion to make their personal lives happier, so they can better focus on their careers. The irresistible work environment encompasses all of these aspects:

- Company culture
- Opportunities for growth and advancement

- Opportunities for additional training and ongoing learning in the current job
- Work-life balance and flexibility (agreeable work hours and working from home)
- Choice of benefits package and extras therein
- Wellness and well-being programs
- Opportunities, criteria and timeliness for promotions
- Leadership training opportunities
- Working on special projects or international assignments
- Opportunities to interact directly with customers
- Job sharing or job shadowing in another department to see if it is interesting work
- One-on-one meetings with the CEO or the leadership team

This is just a partial list, and it should be presented that way—with the caveat that if employees request the development of a new program or benefit and can show how it supports both personal and business objectives, you are open to these innovations. Organizations operating under a Potluck Culture have managers who love to have these conversations about pay. They have had the conversations about their own pay opportunities and, thus, are prepped and ready to share their experiences with others. Addressing hard topics and problem solving are some of the benefits of an effective Potluck Culture.

Intrinsic Motivations

Although intrinsic motivation won't buy food or pay the rent, it does serve very well to engage people in their work. Moreover, when there is no competition from pressing economic demands or other basic psychological needs, creativity can be more easily unleashed. Taking money off the table in a manner that respects the individual's intellect and explains compensation thoroughly clearly focuses people more on intrinsic rewards, including having autonomy in their work.

Famed basketball coach, John Wooden, of the University of California Los Angeles (UCLA) used to say, *"It is amazing how much can be accomplished if no one cares who gets the credit."* Rewards and punishments that go with them are often thought of in terms of *extrinsic* motivators—incentives that go beyond, or are greater than, the task itself and are offered up by someone other than those performing the task. This form of motivating others, sadly, is the norm in the workplaces of today. However, in companies that unleash a Potluck Culture in the modern workplace, the focus is much more on the *intrinsic* motivators.

Harvard University professor, Dr. Teresa Amabile, in her article "Social Influences on Creativity: The Effects of Contracted-For Rewards," posited that "people are intrinsically motivated to engage in a particular task if they view their task engagement as motivated primarily by their own interest and involvement in the task."[2] Therefore, does a paycheck, cash incentive, salary bonus, raise or promotion encourage people to put in more work or work better? We used to all believe that was the case. Well, in a Potluck Culture, substantiated by Dr. Amabile's ground-breaking research, the results suggests otherwise. Rewards, or even more drastic, the threat of punishment, actually make work less enjoyable and perhaps even undermine productivity.

These extrinsic elements can give the illusion that people are more motivated to work harder, but generally, employees who are offered financial rewards tend to, according to Dr. Amabile, "choose easier tasks, are less efficient in using the information available to solve novel problems, and tend to be answer oriented and more illogical in their problem-solving strategies. They seem to work harder and produce activity, but the activity is of a lower quality, contains more errors, and is more stereotyped and less creative than the work of comparable non-rewarded subjects working on the same problem."[3]

OK. So what is our lesson learned here and why do companies operating in a Potluck Culture agree with Dr. Amabile? Perhaps a goal of companies should be to get the best out of their employees by taking money off the table and, therefore, shifting from extrinsic motivation to intrinsic. This, in turn, will build teams of people who are self-motivated by the tasks themselves, inspired by the vision or mission of the organization, rather than by the promise of a paycheck, a bonus or a raise.

Companies can *take money off the table* and engage their employees in a people-driven culture by aligning company practices to motivate people to do the right things and involving employees in the alignment process. Here is a quick survey that companies (likely taken by the company's HR leadership and senior management) can use to gauge their employees' level of motivation in a Potluck Culture:

1. We deploy tools to assess and understand the values, motivations, and talents of our employees. [Yes or No]

2. We thoroughly explain all of our rewards programs to our employees and test to see how good we are at doing so and how well our employees understand them. [Yes or No]

3. We ensure that our employees consider their jobs rewarding, satisfying, and interesting. [Yes or No]

4. We believe that we are a company whose employees are committed to jointly owned, shared goals, values, and beliefs. [Yes or No]

5. We ensure that our employees hold each other accountable to agreed-upon plans and standards. [Yes or No]

6. We revel in having an open and honest communication that empowers our employees. [Yes or No]

Compensation is more than just the amount of a paycheck. It can be worrisome and troubling for employees if they don't know this well. It is incumbent upon companies and their leaders to take money off the table, so the focus can shift to the care and well-being of the employees—holistically.

Chapter 6

STRATEGY #4
INNOVATE AS A HABIT

"There is no doubt that creativity is the most important human resource of all. Without creativity, there would be no progress, and we would be forever repeating the same patterns."

—Dr. Edward de Bono, esteemed management scientist

Aristotle once famously said, "We are what we repeatedly do. Excellence, then, is not an act, but a habit."[1] How uncanny! He recognized that the more people do certain things, the more they follow certain patterns and norms. He noted that this eventually influences who we are as people, how we are wired, what shapes our outlook and how we perceive the world around us. Potluck Cultures recognize this and make it a natural part of work.

Under such a workplace culture, companies realize that people are defined by what they repeatedly do. Well, if that's the case, then we should be darn good at what we spend most of our time doing in the workplace. It is no wonder, then, that in the workplace we are great at administrative tasks, as meeting planners (God only knows how much time we spend in meetings), and as phenomenal cutters of costs and people. When the company does not do well, we are wired to cut costs and even lay off people—sometimes mercilessly.

These poor habits have become ingrained in the workplace, and those organizations that want to break the mold (under a Potluck Culture) want to ingrain habits of innovation and creativity instead. They want to make innovation intentional, link it to the company's strategy and make it valuable and purposeful by integrating it into the jobs of the people they employ. Not only will such an approach unleash a culture of innovation and continually bud creative employees, the practice, itself, honors people and the beauty of their minds. Given the opportunity, people will rise to the challenge and innovate or, at the very least, find ways to break the mold.

Creating Diversity of Talent and Ideology

A diverse workforce does, indeed, create an environmental and organizational climate ripe for innovation. The dialogues, interactions, and exchange of thoughts and experiences are valuable sources of creativity. Facilitated and led by Boomers and Gen Xers, a vital foundation is established for encouraging new ideas, inventions, and better ways to perform work and generate value for customers. The diversity of talent provides more ideas and perspectives for driving the best business solutions. Engaging Millennials in a diverse workforce, in coordination with Boomer and Gen Xer leaders, can become a cherished new tradition and innovative resource.

Research has shown that diverse teams outperform teams composed of only the very best individuals (the so-called high potentials) because a diversity of perspectives and problem-solving approaches wins over individual contributions. In a Potluck Culture, companies naturally channel diverse ideologies, experiences, outlooks, and points of view through dialogue and conversation.

People see problems and solutions from different perspectives. Most employees are energized when collaborating to solve problems through listening, decoding, and exploring ideas. Including all ideologies in such discussions can generate innovation in ways never before seen in the workplace, especially with the intellectually curious, Millennial mindset. There is no better forum for developing them into future leaders to fill the upcoming leadership void.

Establishing Openness and Trust

In a Potluck Culture, people who bring their best and most creative delectable dishes to the table also bring open minds. This sense of inquiry and curiosity is essential for innovation, and companies that allow these to manifest will win.

On the other hand, the quickest way to eradicate curiosity is for organizations to focus inward and spend little time out in the world, particularly with their customers or potential markets. A value system based on openness, empathy for others, and respect for all people that also challenges the status quo will provide the fuel necessary to build habitual innovation.

Moreover, a value system and organizational culture based on creating avenues of trust and opportunities to take risks also drive innovation. Tim Brown, CEO of the Palo Alto, California-based design consultancy IDEO, said the following on building creative mindsets and innovative cultures:

> We tend, in our operationally-minded view of the world, to try and mitigate and design out as much risk as we can, but if you want to innovate, you have to take risks. And to take risks you have to have some level of trust within the organization—because if people get penalized for failure, particularly the kind of failure that's most useful (which is when you learn a lot)—then they're not going to do it. In that case, you're not going to get any innovation.[2]

Connecting with Others in Meaningful Ways

When I was a university professor, I taught MBA students about building leadership skills. The skill that I spent the greatest amount of time on was empathy. Creating unique and ideal solutions requires critical understanding of the problem from the customer's viewpoint. Managing people effectively can only be done if you know how they feel and what they want. How do people in the workplace develop their ability to appreciate and understand the needs of others? To do this, they need imagination—and empathy.

Recently, I was asked to make a presentation about innovation. The sponsors of the event knew of my university days, when I taught a management course entitled "Leadership and Imagination." They wanted to learn how to build creative minds and enable a culture of innovation. Before accepting the speaking engagement, I asked them if I could speak about how to build empathetic skills as opposed to innovation skills. They respectfully agreed to do so, but I could sense a bit of confusion and concern because the event was about innovation.

Empathetic skills enable an emotional as well as a practical understanding of the customer's or employee's problem. Most importantly, empathy allows us to appreciate what someone is going through. Companies that want to remain relevant and continually innovate must include empathy as a leadership skill.

I have had the fortune to have worked for and collaborated with some of the world's most amazing companies. My biggest "aha" during these wonderful times was that companies prosper when they're able to create widespread empathy for the world around them. Companies such as Google, Zappos, LinkedIn, Intuit, Amazon, and Starbucks all are examples of great companies that have benefited from building a culture of widespread empathy for the people they serve. They all have some semblance of a Potluck Culture, and they honor and respect people and what they have to offer.

Every one of us understands empathy on an individual level: the ability to reach outside of ourselves and walk in someone else's shoes, to get where they're coming from, to feel what they feel. Pervasive empathy, or demonstrating empathy as a habit, is about getting every single person in an organization to have a shared and intuitive sense for what's going on in the world, what others have as ideas, and the experiences they have gone through.

Developing a Culture of Innovation

The world's most innovative companies have purposefully built cultures where people are coming up with new ideas all the time.

POTLUCK CULTURE

As in bringing a dish to a potluck dinner, people share ideas and proudly tell how they came up with them and what they signify. Profound learning comes out of settings such as these.

I love music of all kinds. I grew up exposed to all types of music but started the love affair with the melodies of the legendary British upstarts—the Beatles. Steve Jobs, legendary CEO and visionary, also loved the Beatles. He said of the group:

> My model for business is the Beatles. They were four guys who kept each other's kind of negative tendencies in check. They balanced each other, and the total was greater than the sum of the parts. That's how I see business: Great things in business are never done by one person; they're done by a team of people.[3]

Innovation needs time and space to develop and synthesize into tangible outcomes. In most companies, it typically feels like no one ever has time to spare. People get so consumed with putting out fires and chasing short-term targets that most can't even think about the future, let alone innovate. Here is where a Potluck Culture can be most helpful. After all, what organization in the world wants to be irrelevant or become stagnant?

Giving up control when the pressure is greatest is the ultimate innovation contradiction. In a Potluck Culture (as practiced by iconic companies and brands such as 3M, Virgin America, Alibaba, and Google), companies give their employees about ten percent of their work day as "free time" to experiment with new ideas.[4] The software company Atlassian emboldens their employees to take "FedEx Days"—paid days off to work on any problem they want. Of course, just like FedEx, they must deliver something of value twenty-four hours later.[5]

Other companies that follow a similar culture, such as Intuit, use time as a reward because they believe it's the biggest motivator for unleashing creative minds. Intuit gives its best business innovators three months of "unstructured" time that can be used in one big chunk or spread out over six months for part-time exploration of new opportunities.[6] Using time wisely creates a major incentive to get more time to "play" with. These companies have easily recognizable brands, and the single biggest reason why is that they honor people and what they bring to the table. They believe that given the opportunity, time, space and the right culture, they will deliver!

So, how does a Potluck Culture enable innovation as a habit? The following four are some things to consider in your organization:

1. Allow and honor failure.

It is absolutely OK to test ideas, see them fail and honor those who tried. Instead of the usual admonishments at the end of the year to assess their performance, those who tried and failed should be praised and encouraged to continue. This is healthy for organizations, so long as these failures are done with honesty and respect for the company's values and does not undermine any individual or team.

Organizational leaders who are experienced should empower their people—particularly their promising talent—to be entrepreneurial and to intentionally pursue their ideals. If people in the company are worried that their jobs will be in jeopardy if they mess up, then they will <u>never take the risks</u> necessary to develop a stellar concept. A culture of innovation would never materialize or, at best, would only deliver mediocre results.

The only way to ensure true growth and continuous ingenuity is to allow people to try new approaches continuously. This shows your company rewards the process of trial and error, even when there are more errors than successes.

Furthermore, sharing details about missteps openly augments the notion that your company practices what it preaches.

2. Enable teams to collaborate.

Discovering how people best fit within your company and within a team unleashes innovation. The older generation does not always need to feel that they are in charge. Boomers and Gen Xers should provide their employees the room to explore and find their passion. Effective leadership is about delegating and being able to trust yourself enough to let go and allow others to establish their own footing without being so dependent upon you.

Too often, companies try to enable collaboration through an articulated employee value proposition, that is, the return that organizations give to employees for their hard work. Employee engagement isn't enough. It's about allowing employees to be passionate about their work without being too confined to their immediate roles and responsibilities. The passionate worker is always looking to create impact through long-term, sustainable growth. Experienced leaders are the ones who allow their emerging, direct-report talent to discover their passion.

Breaking down organizational silos by inspiring people with different backgrounds and experiences to share their unique perspectives and work in different functional areas is a best practice. Many organizations claim to do this, but even if they do so, this practice is not enabled correctly or with confidence. Becoming a matrix organization (not making it complex, though) can spur the horizontal flow of skills and information transcending functional areas.

A matrix organization uses a structure where there are multiple reporting lines—that is, people have more than one formal boss or supervisor. For example, the matrix organizational structure may divide authority both by functional area (e.g., marketing, IT or HR) and by project (people from various functions working on a company-wide initiative). Each employee answers to two immediate supervisors: a functional supervisor and a project supervisor. The functional supervisor is charged with overseeing employees in a functional area, such as marketing or engineering. Project supervisors manage a specific and often impermanent project. They absorb employees from various functional areas to complete their project teams.

Cross-functional projects, enriched career opportunities, high-visibility projects, direct customer interaction, global assignments and working directly with the chief executive officer are examples of a company's commitment to developing associates through collaborative opportunities. Experienced leaders can share their knowledge and experiences and allow their Millennial stars to grow and develop.

3. Bring back Skunk Works and unleash think tanks.

Great teams require great leadership, and companies can unearth this greatness from its core of existing leaders, who bring years of experience and a depth of organizational know-how. Skunk Works is a group of people who work on special projects in unconventional ways, skirting organizational and managerial structures with the sole purpose of unearthing innovation. This approach needs to be embraced and implemented again and staffed with Millennials under the tutelage of experienced Boomers and Gen Xers.

Skunk Works would create an environment where great ideas can surface and grow and where different channels (as opposed to silos) are solicited for ideas. The ability to act on diverse ideas can direct the growth of a company and help its customers generate value. Such potential game-changing ideas include a Skunk Works mentality and think tank operations.

Old and new leaders can participate in these think tanks as facilitators and thought leaders, guided by clusters of strategic topics that roll up to specific organizational goals and objectives. Boomers and Gen Xers can provide the influence without controlling the dialogue and collaboration. In the modern workplace, their responsibility is to find interconnection points between each cluster to guide focus and thinking. These leaders encourage the younger generation and allow team building to become more organic, less instructional and more enabled by the members of the team themselves.

Leaders should measure effectiveness by how well each member is contributing to the overall thinking, dialogue and impact of the group. Feedback should be almost instant and positive. In today's fast-paced, complex and ever-transforming marketplace, engaging Millennials and discovering their passions are best achieved when they feel valued and empowered to think, act and innovate in ways that come most naturally to them.

Google, Amazon, Nike, Apple, Ford Motors, IBM, Samsung, and Nordstrom's (to name just a few companies) are reinstalling the flavor and value of Skunk Works or labs. Lockheed Martin, the first company to do this, had a facility that started in a tent next to a putrid manufacturing plant. That tiny space designed and built America's first jet fighter in just 143 days, and created a philosophy for rapid innovation, which many companies copy to this day.[7]

Now, as companies have to do more with less people, many are moving away from giant research centers and towards building something like a lean startup inside their companies. The companies that do this have a Potluck Culture where they resource and staff such labs as a reward for employees who have accomplished good things or show a propensity for imagination and creativity. Of course, there are a lot more techniques and tools used to make these centers successful, but the mainstay is a focus on people who have the interest, ingenuity, and fortitude to work autonomously to achieve great things for the company. Failures and mistakes in such environments are honored and used as learning opportunities to advance the cause of the company.

4. Teach self-management.

Arguably, the single biggest gift that the elder statesmen of today's workplace can give to their future leaders is coaching on building self-awareness and, in general, how to self-manage. Self-management is the ability to prioritize goals and be accountable to complete the necessary actions. Millennials love to work when they feel like working. Therefore, it can appear that they may not possess the discipline to self-manage. The older generation of leaders like structure and established work hours. Millennials shun this approach, but it does not mean that they shun responsibility and work. That said, each generation must learn to appreciate one another, with the reverence tilting toward the

Millennials who yearn to be a part of Potluck Cultures and who constantly crave feedback to boost their self-awareness and performance.

In today's complex work environment of a multigenerational workforce, the need for quality self-management is at unprecedented levels. More work will be done remotely, and all those wanting to be in leadership roles will be required to continually build their self-awareness. Table 4 shows what senior leaders can do for their subordinates who will ultimately succeed them.

Table 4. Self-management

Self-Management Leadership Behaviors	What Today's Workplaces Can Offer
Encourage self-goal setting Encourage self-observation Encourage self-regulation Encourage self-expectation Encourage self-criticism	Challenging work Advice and counsel from experience Culture of dialogue and inclusion Freedom to try and fail Autonomy in work

Make it competitive through recognition and rewards.

What gets measured gets done. All-employee events, just as in school-sponsored science fairs, can be held in which employees present their creative ideas and the best entry is selected. Given the opportunity, people will bring their best to the table. Prizes or rewards should be offered, not just for the winning entry, but for those that have potential.

Incorporating such behaviors into the company's performance review will ensure that innovation and experimentation are rewarded as essential attributes. It will signal that everyone's ideas matter. Stories of teams and individuals who participated and were rewarded should be shared across the company with photos of them innovating at work. Everyone in the company should know what type of company they work for.

One of my favorite comedians, John Cleese, the British entertainer famous for the Monty Python series, once pontificated about how the human mind works. He said this,

> We all operate in two contrasting modes, which might be called open and closed. The open mode is more relaxed, more receptive, more exploratory, more democratic, more playful and more humorous. The closed mode is the tighter, more rigid, more hierarchical, and operating with tunnel vision.

> Most people unfortunately spend most of their time in the closed mode. Not that the closed mode cannot be helpful. If you are leaping a ravine, the moment of takeoff is a bad time for considering alternative strategies. When you charge the enemy machine-gun post, don't waste energy trying to see the funny side of it. Do it in the 'closed' mode. But the moment the action is over, try to return to the 'open' mode—to open your mind again to all the feedback from our action that enables us to tell whether the action has been successful, or whether further action is needed to improve on what we have done. In other words, we must return to the open mode, because in that mode we are the most aware, most receptive, most creative, and therefore at our most intelligent.[8]

So how do we enable a climate where the "open mode" is unleashed in people and they bring their most creative and most intelligent selves to the table? Trust is the first domino to tip and create a chain reaction if a company wants to make innovation a habit. If leaders are unwilling to create it, live it, demonstrate it, or incorporate it into their routines, then a people-driven culture cannot live and breathe.

In a Potluck Culture, where people are free to ideate and share opinions openly and without repercussions, trust is an essential ingredient for making innovation a habit. People work together to support one another through the process, often at the cost of some personal sacrifice. That's the nature of enabling trust.

Google has built a mammoth organization that continually innovates. Google's founder, Sergey Brin, believes that one reason for this monumental success is that the company believes (as a core competency) that innovation comes from anywhere. There are no jobs that have a title with the word *innovation* in it. It's a role that everyone participates in. Failure in this company is known fondly as a badge of honor. They playfully say that they want to have great people working for them and it's OK that sometimes they fail gracefully.[9]

Successful, innovative companies also give their employees time to get away from their daily tasks, to work on personal or company projects not directly related to their work, helping them *tap into the creative process*. Google, for example, recently deployed a work concept they call "20% time." This type of workplace technique—aligned well to Potluck Cultures—gives employees one day each week to pursue anything that fuels their interests and passions. For example, employees could take the time—with the blessings of their managers—to learn a new skill or participate in a charitable event on the company's time, or even challenge the status quo of a particular process they want to change.[10]

Similarly, 3M Corp has apportioned fifteen percent of its employees' time to work on projects that may be the precursor of a new product or service. It is this type of reverence for allowing employees to work on their passionate peeves that resulted in the advent of the now-famous yellow sticky note.[11] These companies thrive in a Potluck Culture and continue to remain relevant and, in many cases, continue to be revered brands.

Famed speaker and author Daniel Pink said that when innovation gets postponed for too long, companies deteriorate. He posited that "innovation programs remove the constraints that accompany traditional work, and offer a safe space for failure that lets people try riskier things."[12] Reward employees with time to think, while providing them with the structure they need. A Potluck Culture allows such an environment.

The modern workplace is changing before our eyes, and more and more companies are realizing this and riding this wave of change. Old and bad habits are being shunned, and a focus on people and their innate, unfettered, and limitless capabilities is being explored and encouraged. To do this well, innovation needs to be intentional and an integral part of the company's culture. Futuristic thinkers should be developed by leaders of the company. These leaders need to couple innovation to corporate strategy and make it valuable and purposeful. In Potluck Cultures—where people are allowed and expected to bring their best to the table—innovation is a habit. Only in such cultures will innovation be as easy and as acceptable as doing business as usual.

Organizations must move away from the days where they developed managers to be efficiency experts. Many of them have progressed onwards into the management ranks—unknowingly unleashing *efficiency* as a habit. In the modern workplace, these skills have to be rebalanced and reset where the expectation is both efficiency and *innovation*. Heed the concept proposed by Aristotle, rephrased here: Innovation is a competency that must be practiced regularly for it to be ingrained as part of the norm.

Chapter 7

STRATEGY #5
MAKE WORK MEANINGFUL

"The people who get on in this world are the people who get
up and look for the circumstances they want, and,
if they can't find them, make them."

—George Bernard Shaw

I used to poll my students with the question, "How many of you are satisfied in your job?" In the three years I taught, out of an average of twenty students per class, only two hands ever went up. Why are most people in the workplace so unhappy at work? While there are many contributors to this, let's look at the primary reasons why people work. They want to

- earn enough money to make a good living,
- progress and achieve an element of status or success,
- make a difference to the strategic outcomes of their company,
- fulfill an ambition or follow a passion, or
- utilize their skills and talents.

This list did not result from rocket science or deep thinking. These are simple interests—human aspirations. Organizational leaders need to address the wellbeing of their own employees, the people who are already working under their banner and wear the uniform of the company. Companies can address these needs through people programs and processes, such as performance management, talent and succession management, pay for performance, and learning and development. Yet many organizations often dehumanize these processes by not involving the employees in their design, delivery, and success.

> While successful organizations are focused on the business of work
> and the value they offer their marketplaces and customers,
> those that make meaningful experiences for their employees
> will separate themselves from the rest and win effortlessly.

Table 5 shows some ways you can significantly improve these traditional people processes in a Potluck Culture.

Table 5. How to enhance the people process

People Process	How to Enhance the Process
Performance Management	· Take the fear out of performance management. · Focus on multiple years of performance. · Emphasize behaviors, not just results. · Make it part of a conversation (culture of dialogue). · Conduct throughout the year and not as a year-end event. · Eliminate ratings and labeling people with numbers. · Integrate with other people processes (e.g., pay). · Build a culture around performance management.
Talent Management	· Focus on key leadership skills. · Identify jobs that are mission critical. · Spread this process over three years. · Integrate with other people processes (e.g., recruiting). · Include all or most employees (those deep within the company). · Build a culture around talent management.
Succession Management	· Ensure the CEO attends and sponsors. · Include all or most employees (those deep within the company). · Focus on critical positions. · Integrate with other people processes (e.g., talent). · Build a culture around succession management. · Let people know where they stand.
Pay for Performance	· Demystify pay. · Build well-being or wellness programs. · Build a culture around pay for performance. · Explain how all pay elements can have "at risk" elements. · Integrate with other people processes (e.g., learning). · Focus on all rewards (including learning).
Learning and Development	· Identify key leadership skills needed for the company. · Ensure everyone gets trained. · Train through experiential learning. · Integrate with other people processes (e.g., pay). · Build a culture around learning and development.

These processes are much needed in today's multigenerational work-force where Millennials are in the prime position to emerge as future leaders. Meaningful work comes from one of the building blocks of organizational flexibility and instills a sense of resilience in future leaders. Emerging leaders need help connecting the dots. In other words, when they believe what they do has a positive purpose within the organization, as well as to customers and, most of all, to the world, they are connected to their values and ideals.

The older generation plays a critical role in making these connections for their future leaders. Helping young employees be more connected to a group of people whose lives are enhanced makes for a far better work climate where collaboration can lead to productive results. As a leader, you essentially build a pipeline of talent connected to all facets of the company's purpose and direction. This pipeline will be full of engaged and committed emerging leaders who will build on this.

Developing such connections at work helps build leadership resilience; the higher the level of connections, the greater the resilience. The outcomes of this synergy are priceless: reduced workplace stress (particularly in tough times) and increased self-confidence for employees who, in turn, feel more secure about their lives. Great pay or challenging work will not make up for the lack of collaboration. Therefore, experienced leaders helping the emerging ones to make connections and find their paths to purpose is an alignment worth exploring for companies today.

Help Employees Define Success

Most people who look for jobs rarely consider how it adds meaning to their lives. In the early days of my career, I realized that without finding meaning in my work, I was miserable, distrusting of my bosses, unwilling to collaborate, and genuinely dissatisfied with my job. The practical implications of this conflicting behavior can be seen in almost every company.

Connecting employees' passions and personal interests with their work motivates them to work harder and care more about their work. The connection reduces their stress levels, regardless of their workload, and makes them feel more successful. Organizational leaders need to take note of this phenomenon as it is clearly an opportunity to engage people in meaningful ways.

Employees often lack clarity in identifying work that will connect to what matters deeply to them and provide them with a sense of meaning and purpose. Although they are certain of the importance and positive impact doing meaningful work would have on their career and personal lives, most of them haven't yet discovered what they should be doing to derive that sense of purpose. There is a fertile opportunity for companies to help their employees identify what matters to them and how it can be tied to what they do as members of their organization. In doing so, leaders will provide talent development that will ensure employees remain invested in their organization's shared purpose.

In my career, I have worked at three semiconductor companies—of which at one, I was the Chief HR Officer. In these companies, where the core of employees was engineers, it was hard to find women in leadership positions. First, there weren't many women who had graduated from college engineering programs. As the chief leader of people, I wanted to find a way to break this mold but struggled to find a solution. Then I met Angie, a young engineer who had great ambitions.

One day, Angie asked if I could have coffee with her. Of course, I obliged but was a little concerned as to what the topic was. When we met, she confessed that she was feeling terribly conflicted, depressed, and lost at the time, not knowing where her life and work were going. I listened intently. She told me that she had read a lot on meaning, purpose, and personal values to discover what it was that actually drove and motivated her.

During our conversation, Angie came to the realization that she wanted to advance in her career at a fast pace but was unsure as to where it would take her, given the company's poor record of placing women in senior leadership positions. She recognized that her purpose in life had much to do with empowering women. She said to me, "It's been a recurring theme in my life. But while there are many ways to help empower women, I need to find the one way that actually 'speaks' to me and my job and how I connect it to my work."

As a result, Angie started a grassroots initiative—on her own time—to form a Women's Leadership Network at our company. I agreed to champion the cause and eventually even found some budget money to help the fledgling organization have meaningful gatherings and invite guest speakers. And with this, Angie found purpose and meaning in her work.

Recently, I spoke with Angie and she told me that she had been promoted to Senior Director. Her HR leadership regularly calls on her to participate in company events with the goal of making a meaningful career in an otherwise male-dominated industry. "I don't know how long this whole thing will be a part of my life, but it certainly has given me meaning and purpose. I do know, though, that whatever follows will also be about empowering women and, for me, that's very reassuring to know."

Millennials and Purpose in Work

Millennials, who will soon form the backbone of the world's workplaces, need help to find meaning in their work. They yearn for it and insist on it. Experienced leaders can help Millennials identify what matters most to them and what they desire to experience. This could be a customer experience, the chance to design a product, brand a service offering, name a website or suggest taglines for company events.

Linking personal feelings and integrating personal goals into work goals creates a powerful combination. Moreover, it may be useful to understand the background and upbringing of future leaders. Appreciating and asking how their families and circle of friends inspired them, what shaped their mindsets, what their expectations are for their company and their managers and, most of all, what motivates them to work are all queries that experienced leaders can use to engage their Millennial coworkers.

Success is not always shaped by work-related accomplishments for Millennials. They care more about the influences they can have and, just as importantly, what influence their organizations can have on the communities they live in. Experienced leaders need to really think big here. They should reflect on their impact to the local community, at the state and national level and also on a global scale. All these dimensions are of critical importance in today's workplace. Organizational leaders should ask what problems they could help solve. Millennials could help participate in these noble ventures, which will do nothing but drive up shareholder value and respect for the companies themselves.

Millennials should also be asked to reflect on what they feel most aligned with in terms of the company's core values. It would be a fallacy to think that all employees believe in every single value of the company they work for. Millennials, in particular, are not that easily influenced. Therefore, their managers should inquire as to why they are in the company and what their eventual motive to stay is. At the same time, they can find out what projects or outcomes resonate most strongly with those values. It would also be wise to ask Millennials what one thing their leaders can do to make these activities a greater part of their lives.

Connecting to purposeful work might take serious effort and soul-searching on the parts of all generations in the diverse workforce, but doing so thoughtfully will foster less stress and greater motivation at work. As an added bonus, perhaps, this thoughtfulness can even help make the world a better place.

If you don't like the news, go make some of your own.

Twenty years ago, I used to listen to a San Francisco-based radio show every Friday at 4:59 p.m., right at the onset of happy hour and the beginning of the weekend. The show was a minute-long rundown of the day's headline news and ended with the announcer, Wes "Scoop" Nisker, proclaiming, "If you don't like the news you just heard, then go out and make some of your own!"

How timely this advice is today. It's more important than ever to have a story to tell because people don't just buy products—they buy the stories behind the products and the companies that make them. We see it daily on social media and in advertising campaigns that tug at our heartstrings. In Potluck Cultures, stories about employees, teams, customers, and vendors abound and are audible everywhere. In such cultures, people are invited and encouraged to think about human elements, the deep connections they make with one another, and factors that reveal themselves in how content is created. This is because the story is all about people and the relationships between them.

Storytelling is powerful. It causes people to be engaged *at* work and *with* their work. It helps companies brand themselves by telling the world how they got to where they are. It helps rally change management efforts, build teams, and promote camaraderie. Most importantly, it connects companies and their products to their customers.

People don't just buy a company's product. Rather, they buy the stories behind those products. Most significantly, every story exists in relationship to everything else around it, and nowhere is it more in full bloom and in evidence than in actual potluck settings. People playfully brag about the stories behind the food they brought to the table and what inspired them to do so. More and more organizations are following this news announcer's inspiring words, realizing that the stories they tell are critical to attracting customers.

So what do you do if your company doesn't have a story to tell, or if the story you do have isn't resonating with your customers and employees? Here are three easy ways to begin developing your company's new beginning.

Start with "Imagine if ..."

Everyone likes "once upon a time" stories, but "imagine if" stories can be powerfully shaped and nurtured. Imagining your company's ideal future is a great place to start. A good example of this is CVS

Pharmacy. CVS leaders decided to rebrand their company to promote and effuse everything related to health. Its new name, CVS Health, says it all. They wanted to reflect a broader health care commitment by helping people on their path to better health. The company stopped selling cigarettes in its retail stores and offers onsite clinics and wellness programs, including alternative health therapies and products.[1] The Company didn't like its story, so it went out and made its own news.

Try saying, "We get excited by ..."

To help your company continue to develop the direction of its story, try stating how excited you are about a change, trend, or event that's happening in your industry. A recent example of this is Domino's, which recently dropped the word "Pizza" from its name. It realized that selling a variety of tasty foods rather than just pizza, which they already were doing well, was something that needed to be storied. It has rebranded itself to an outfit that wants to be known as the premier, fast-food service provider.[2] They imagined a new future, so they went out and made their own news.

Thinking futuristically like this will begin to shape ideas that will help propel your story forward. Ten years later, everyone will be talking about your story as they contemplate buying your products.

Use the stories of your employees.

Your employees are the keepers of your culture, and because of this, their stories will generally showcase the company's story as well. Begin documenting one or more of your company's leaders or even your rising stars. They are likely in the process of building the story that will determine your company's future. Think about how they think and behave, whom they connect with and how they do it, how they build followers, and what drives and motivates them.

An example of this is David Tran, CEO of Huy Fong Foods, the makers of Sriracha Hot Chili Sauce. An immigrant chili farmer from Vietnam, Tran came to the United States as a refugee on a ship called the *Huy Fong* (the inspiration for the company's name) and built his American dream. Tran humbly said that he never intended to become a billionaire and only wanted to "make enough fresh chili sauce so that everyone who wants Huy Fong can have it. Nothing more."[3] The company has rallied around this compelling immigration story and continues to be successful.

What these three approaches have in common is an underlying emotion, a sense of curiosity that invites people to make real connections with their companies and continually draws in customers. When telling future vision stories, start with an invitation and the possibility of what could be. If you do it well and purposefully, customers will come.

> Workplace stories engage people, build teams, and promote camaraderie. They help manage change, reduce the negative impact of economic downturns, cut through the noise, and are vehicles to model good behavior.

Millennials, who are rushing into the modern workplace at a breakneck pace, are wired for stories more than any previous generation. Traditionalists, Boomers, and Gen Xers have lots of stories to tell. With a willing audience of eager-eyed Millennials wanting to hear them, it is vital that business storytelling becomes part of the culture of modern organizations. People want to hear the stories that made companies and leaders what they are today.

Chapter 8

SCRUMPTIOUSLY WRAPPING IT ALL UP

"Never tell people how to do things. Tell them what to do and they will surprise you with their ingenuity."

—General George S. Patton Jr., United States Army

Organizations today need to respond to their environments much more resourcefully and intelligently. The ever-changing world of work has increased the stakes to unprecedented levels, requiring organizations to respond more quickly. While this increased speed has led to tremendous gains in the ability of businesses to take advantage of new markets and consumers, it has also created a workforce that is overworked, underappreciated, increasingly confused, disenfranchised, and out of touch with the fundamental values that matter most to them and even to the organizations they are a part of.

In his book, *Employees First, Customers Second*, HCL Technologies' CEO, Vineet Nayar, spoke of a company he envisioned and eventually established and led. His employee-first philosophy led to the creation of a highly successful company where he oversaw the unleashing of a sense of urgency by enabling employees to see the truth of his company's current state, as well as feel the "romance" of its possible future. He tapped into the nebulous arena of building trust by an open-kimono communication and information-sharing strategy.[1]

Nayar inverted the organizational hierarchy by making management and the enabling functions accountable to the employees first and not to shareholders or even the company's customers. Most significantly, he unlocked the potential in all HCL's employees by fostering an entrepreneurial mindset, decentralizing decision-making and transferring the ownership of driving, harnessing and managing change to his greatest asset—the company's people.

A culture of shared success can be positive and powerfully poignant when all stakeholders, including employees, are involved. A Potluck Culture revolves around the employee and is created with the employee in mind. A good lesson can be learned from Huntsman Cancer Institute. This company has built a workplace for their customers *by* their employees. They don't use consulting firms to tell them what to do nor rely on seniority and senior executives to strategize about what customers need. Instead they turned to their most prized assets—their people—to show the way.

Jobs in the institute are designed by those in it. Employees empathetically develop them with the organization's mission firmly in their minds. They design them in a manner where the employee can do the best job for their cancer-stricken patients. They are also in charge of what their workplace looks like, everything from the types of plants and carpeting to what goes into the game rooms and what food is served in the cafeterias. They design the jobs and the workplace with the holistic patients in mind so as to ease their suffering. They include the patients' families in their thought process.[2] Given the opportunity, people will rise to the occasion and bring their best to the table.

When I was working at a financial services company in a downtown high-rise building, days after the unforgettable horror that took place in New York, Pennsylvania and Washington on 9-11, I noticed that each floor's leading administrative assistant, without prompting, took the lead to develop lean processes for evacuation and safety. They assembled themselves, developed a project plan, and executed it with aplomb. Each month they measured the success of the new process, so that in the event history repeats itself, people can save themselves. Given the opportunity to be autonomous in their work, people will rise to the challenge and accomplish great things.

Investing in a Potluck Culture can be easily followed by any company so long as they do so with a truthful and authentic focus on people. The premise is that a nurturing, collaborative, respectful, people-focused, and human culture—all linked to the company's strategic goals spearheaded by employees—will lead to increased profitability and greater personal satisfaction.

People-Centered Environments

Even as employees search for meaning, many managers and leaders still put their primary focus on profits, percentages, and production—the wrong Ps. The right P (people) is viewed as secondary, or even lower in priority. To engage the modern workplace, this is just not feasible and certainly not sustainable. To thrive over the long term, leaders must transform their organizations, moving from bureaucratic, profit-centered businesses to empowered, people-centered businesses filled with a positive vibe. When you put your people first, profits will follow.

Every organization needs to be true to its north star, its reason for existence. Each has its own unique culture made up of its values, its attitudes, its history (successes and failures), and its collective consciousness. People-centered leaders working in a Potluck Culture are masters of seeing a true vision of what paths the organization and its members should take to match its culture with its customers, employees and other business partners. Targeting these values can rightly sway the focus toward people and what they are capable of achieving.

While it's true that most businesses exist primarily to make money for their shareholders and owners, for any company to continue to succeed in the future, leaders and management must stop focusing on money and profit at the expense of employees and other business partners. Find ways to honor people through an authentic focus on employees to find the values and behaviors that really count—respect, love, authenticity, empathy, and trust. Strike a balance between the company's need to make a profit and the need of employees and other business partners to prosper in both a spiritual and financial sense.

Mentorship matters and in a Potluck Culture, it is a widely utilized management tool. Employees benefit enormously from mentorship, and great leaders make time for this, knowing that it will be a godsend for productivity and effectiveness, not only for those they mentor, but for the entire company. Encouraging self-leadership can help accomplish great things through unleashing the energy within leaders and their teams. No matter where they are in the organization's hierarchy, from the lowest-paid clerk to the highest-paid senior executive, employees must take action themselves and not depend on others to take action on their behalf. In a Potluck Culture, involving employees in the transformational activities that may radically change the company is part of its DNA.

By encouraging cooperation, creating opportunities for teamwork, and making free and open communication a reality instead of simply a goal, companies will not only illuminate a vision of the future, but provide the necessary information and tools to achieve it as well. Enabling every employee to express his or her highest levels of creativity, innovation and productivity is the duty of all leaders. A Potluck Culture demands it and lives by it.

Finally, as a leader, you have a duty to share your knowledge with all the members of the community in which you work.

All great leaders not only give their people the tools they need to create positive change, but they create a body of knowledge that will help others along their own paths in the absence of the leader.

Unless there is something that is absolutely sensitive or private in nature, everything should be shared with employees. This empowers them and makes them feel as though they are an integral part of the company and its mission.

Richard Branson was able to build his company into a global powerhouse by focusing on two key words: customer service. Even though he was a prolific acquirer of other companies, he did not put Virgin's name on that company until it excelled in customer service at the highest level. But don't be fooled by this. I am confident he would be the first to say that Virgin employees are the company's top priority. Branson stated, "It should go without saying, if the person who works at your company is one hundred percent proud of the brand and you give them the tools to do a good job and they are treated well, they're going to be happy."[3]

To ensure that people are cared for, Branson trains his managers and leaders to be wired for empathy, and he personally goes so far as to collect feedback by walking around the cabin and having chats with flight staff during his Virgin flights. Simply put, if people who work at your company are not appreciated, they are not going to do things with a smile.

By not treating employees well, companies risk losing customers over bad service. Happy employees equal happy customers, and in a Potluck Culture, this can be achieved. Cultures such as this honor people, respect their intelligence, and do everything possible to get the best out of them. According to Branson, "Effectively, in the end shareholders do well, the customers do better, and your staff remains happy."[4]

Changing Dynamics

The dynamics of the workplace will change even more in the future. Company leaders will be grappling with engaging their prized assets and developing a strong and deep talent pipeline. Since Millennials will soon form the backbone of the workplace, companies will want to start planning for an intentional workplace cultural shift to ensure that strong collaboration thrives to propel success. It is vital that Millennials are nurtured and the best in them is unveiled and unleashed for the sake of the future of that workplace. It is equally important to ensure that they get along with and strike a positive, productive and profitable relationship with their older counterparts.

Millennials typically are individualistic, innovative celebrators of diversity. They are multitaskers and they write their own rules. They appreciate a structured, supportive work environment where feedback and dialogue are culturally ingrained in the company. They relish job profiles or descriptions that are customized to get the best out of them. These personalized work assignments need to be designed with experienced leaders, managers and supervisors actively involving Millennials in the process.

Millennials work well in a team environment and prefer to have close relationships with their supervisors to help them feel more confident and supported. They can be relied upon to carefully and successfully balance their work and personal lives and are unwilling to commit to jobs requiring long hours, evening, or weekend work. Yet many Millennials *will* go above and beyond because they *want* to.

At the end of the day, Millennials aren't really that different from previous generations. They may be more technologically savvy than their older workplace counterparts and possess different skill sets and priorities, but ultimately, the end goal across generations in the modern workplace is to make a difference, better themselves, earn a living, feel good about their pay and contribute in a way that is meaningful and exciting.

Table 6 shows a summary of what drives people (with an emphasis on Millennials).

Table 6. Leading, managing, and motivating employees

Motivators Used in Potluck Cultures	
Authentic Leadership	People desire a clear career track linked to performance goals that lets them know how they are doing and encourages them to keep improving. Millennials want their leaders to be role models so they can learn from them and grow. They want frequent interactions with them and expect honest, timely, conversational-type performance feedback.
Collaborative Work	Millennials like working with people and look to coworkers for friendship. Coworkers need an environment where they can share ideas and interact with other, perhaps through regularly scheduled brainstorming sessions and knowledge transfer opportunities.
Fun Workplace	People get stressed easily. Having outlets for them to express joy, laughter and fun releases endorphins in the body that stimulate focus and clarity. All professionals want to look forward to coming to work every day. They thrive in a fun, friendly, creative environment that allows them to work and grow as individuals.
Career Growth	Everyone wants to improve and advance in their careers. They want to adopt and learn new skills. Many desire to become leaders. Customization from managers is important to fit personal needs. Individuals want to learn and be assigned to projects that will help them meet their personal growth goals.
Flexibility and Balance	As the years go by and work gets more demanding, it becomes much harder to balance work and life, and the line between the two has blurred. People desire more flexibility and demonstrated trust from their managers that the work will get done—from wherever it is done. This helps to provide the balance they are looking for and increases their feeling of being valued.

What Employers and Their Existing Leaders Can Do

Appreciate that segmenting your workforce is a vital first step in building, winning, high-performing cultures. Taking a demographic stock of the workforce follows. It's quite important to recognize and address generational differences, motivational needs, likes and dislikes, and what people truly value. In today's world of "big data," using analytics and metrics coupled with benchmark analysis can help segment your workforce to better understand what each generation values, particularly your Millennials.

Organizations should carefully craft the deal, or employee value proposition, to ensure that employee engagement is high. Analyzing the results by workforce demographics can help isolate issues and pinpoint exactly what the remedy needs to be. Results of all-employee surveys can be divided by age group and a predictive analysis used to highlight potential retention issues.

Millennials, by nature, are restless and will easily move to other companies if they feel the need to. Therefore, proactively polling them and analyzing their feedback through such vehicles will shed a bright light on potential issues. Being long-term focused and proactive in talent management is a healthy practice in the complex work world of today.

Make the Deal Meaningful

It's important for employers to explain what they are offering a potential employee, but also what they expect in return. Motivation means different things to different people. A one-size-fits-all approach may have worked in the past, but today, things are different. Thus, thinking creatively about reward strategies and what motivates people needs to be purposeful and deliberate. For example, is it time to shift focus from cash incentives to include other nonfinancial rewards?

Recall that the majority of Millennials are attracted to the prospect of having rewards and benefits designed specifically for them. There is often a significant gap between perception and reality when it comes to the promises made by employers for diversity and work-life balance, causing an inauthentic workplace. If companies want to continue to attract employees, this has to be addressed.

Companies should review the messages they are sending and test them against the reality of the employee experience. Rewards such as meaningful work, challenging projects, contact with senior and important people in the company, direct customer impact, and working on special products will cause the Millennials to salivate at the prospect of participating in these programs.

Grow Them

Managers and leaders in today's world need to really understand the personal and professional goals of workers in the modern workplace. Give them a chance to participate in important conversations. Listen carefully to them, not just for their ideas, but also to help discover the skills they need to hone, competencies they need to build and behaviors they need to demonstrate. Challenge them to come up with new ways to streamline processes and exercise creativity. Coach them that the "same as last year's thinking" is unacceptable and they are relied upon to change the status quo.

For example, Millennials have the most global access of any generation, and they have a genuine interest in other cultures and people of different walks and settings. Therefore, they would appreciate a chance to go on a foreign business trip, work on a short-term project in another country, and possibly move their work overseas. This becomes an even greater proposition for organizations focused on global growth.

If your organization is more focused on developing high potentials, or more senior people, then you could risk losing future talent if you fail to engage Millennials with development opportunities. Millennials want to experience as much training as possible. Build and measure the effectiveness of mentoring programs alongside other learning and education. In addition, every opportunity should also be taken to mix teams generationally. Consider allocating projects to talented Millennials that fall outside their day job. Let them connect, collaborate, build their networks, and, most of all, innovate.

Focus on Conversation

People want and value frequent feedback. Unlike in the past where people received annual reviews, Millennials want to know how they're doing much more regularly. Give them honest feedback in real time and highlight positive contributions or improvements on key competencies.

Workers in the modern workplace also want flexibility. They work well with clear instructions conducted through respectful dialogue and conversation, as well as concrete targets and dates for completion. If you know what you want done by when, why does it matter where and how they complete the task? Productive and talented individuals will get the work done. Just don't expect them to follow a "nine to five" work hour mentality all the time. Give them the freedom to have a flexible work schedule. Of course, set deadlines and if they meet them, don't worry so much about their tactics and the time they clock in and out.

Promote in Creative Ways—and Do It with Haste

Lateral moves should be viewed and positioned as promotions. "Up or out" promotion policies should not be the norm. All employees want to be challenged, and giving them promotions in lateral roles will have a significant motivational impact.

Historically, career advancement was built upon seniority and time of service. However, some individuals are not wired that way. They value results over tenure and are sometimes frustrated with the amount of time it takes to work up the career ladder. Many from the current generation want career advancement much quicker than older generations are accustomed to achieving it. So, for the high achievers who do show the potential to rise up the ranks, they will likely need positive ways to be promoted or recognized.

A relatively simple solution, such as adding more levels, grades, or other "badges," could be enough to meet their expectations. Titles don't cost a thing, but they do build priceless retention tools for organizations.

Always Exit the Poor Performers Gracefully

In a Potluck Culture, exiting a poor performer
can be done with respect and grace.

Because of a sense of guilt, uncertainty about the decision, legal concerns, and hearing excuse after excuse by the team member, many managers don't let poor performers go. However, when they do take action, almost every termination conversation is stressful.

That said, keeping poor performers in the company is a disservice to other team members, customers, the organization and even to the person in question. Lowering standards, even in a people-centric culture, can bring down the aspiration level of other team members. Poor performers often incite resentment. When it is time to let a team member go, knowing how to terminate him or her properly makes managers more confident and compassionate and team members more accepting.

On the flip side, Millennials and Boomers will deeply appreciate a graceful exit, particularly if the proverbial door is left open for them to return. They will pass the message through their vast web of connections to say how generous your company is and what a respectful culture you have. This is a great public relations move for your organization.

Summary Thoughts

Building a people-centric culture requires, above all, an empathetic, common-sense approach paired with up-to-date business savvy. It also requires keeping an eye on the horizon to make sure your company knows what to innovate for. Once you've got your Potluck Culture simmering, make use of these final guidelines to keep your company headed in the right direction, ready with a plan for whatever adaptation you may need:

1. Align your business plan and talent strategy.

Make sure every aspect of your talent strategy directly contributes to your overall business plan and to creating value. Change anything that doesn't. Recognize the importance Millennials will play in your plans.

2. Face the future.

Look at where your business is heading, not where you've been. Keep questioning whether your talent management pipeline will give you what you need when you need it. Consider the part Millennials will play in your future talent needs. Do you have a strategic, people-planning approach in place to help you understand where shortages are likely?

3. Pay attention to pivotal roles.

Get the right talent into the roles that have a disproportionate ability to create (or destroy) business value. Is your succession plan ready to start moving Millennials into these vital roles?

4. Focus on the financials.

Make measurement, benchmarking, and analytics part of your plan. Look to your people's return on investment. Track the cost of replacing lost Millennial talent. What impact will losing talent have on your strategic priorities?

In the end, it's all about people. This old cliché is starting to gain urgency for companies that want to thrive. Great workplace cultures are not born from an accidental convergence of naturally, highly motivated employees. Rather, they are intentionally created by forward-thinking and futuristic-minded leaders. Potluck Cultures are purposefully developed and are not left to chance. It is also more than just a strategic decision to build a workplace; it involves both humanity and integrity.

Potluck Cultures have people-centered leaders who intentionally align and link their philosophy to clients, customers and shareholders. These companies deserve high praise for making the connection between

162

business success and people success. Richard Branson said it best, "My philosophy is put your employees first, your customers second and your investors third and, in the end, everyone will be happy."[5]

Because the stakes are high, we ask our employees to work harder, and they are often told to do more with less. This is all the more reason why we need to honor them and respect their accomplishments. Employees will come through for you if given the opportunity. As in a potluck meal, where the host welcomes everyone, companies invite their employees to bring their best offerings. It is in the spirit of such gatherings where we see the diversity in people and enjoy the dialogues they bring to the table.

> Organizations that revere people and believe without reservation that people are its truest and most powerful asset will thrive in the modern work world.

Building a great workplace goes hand-in-hand with an authentic belief in people. *Every* individual brings something to the table.

Appendix A

POTLUCK CULTURE ASSESSMENT

Potluck Culture Assessment

Use this assessment to build awareness about your company's commitment to an authentic people-centered culture.

There are no right or wrong answers. Select the answer that seems most accurate to you, using this scale:

Strongly Agree	Agree	Undecided	Disagree	Strongly Disagree	Don't Know
⑤	④	③	②	①	⓪

Get the Fit Right — Your Rating

		Your Rating
1	We utilize talent assessment tools in hiring (e.g., DISC, Motivators and Job Profiles).	⑤ ③ ② ① ⓪
2	We onboard new hires gracefully and assimilate them quickly and effectively.	⑤ ③ ② ① ⓪
3	We effectively use social media tools to engage potential new hires and begin the process early.	⑤ ③ ② ① ⓪
4	Management and key leaders regularly participate in recruiting activities.	⑤ ③ ② ① ⓪
5	We have a strategic plan to hire the best and brightest employees.	⑤ ③ ② ① ⓪

165

POTLUCK CULTURE

Build a Culture of Dialogue   **Your Rating**

6	We teach our leaders to lead other leaders as well as self-management.	⑤ ③ ② ① ⓪
7	There is a high degree of trust between management and employees.	⑤ ③ ② ① ⓪
8	Management takes a genuine interest in managing people and their performance.	⑤ ③ ② ① ⓪
9	Performance management focuses on regular feedback, dialogue and conversations (not ratings).	⑤ ③ ② ① ⓪
10	We regularly provide feedback to one another and are grateful for it.	⑤ ③ ② ① ⓪

Take Money off the Table   **Your Rating**

11	We de-mystify all elements of pay and benefits, especially base salary.	⑤ ③ ② ① ⓪
12	We deploy a total rewards strategy and wellness program, and our employees know them well.	⑤ ③ ② ① ⓪
13	We invest purposely in learning and training programs.	⑤ ③ ② ① ⓪
14	We regularly seek feedback on what motivates our employees (and we implement findings).	⑤ ③ ② ① ⓪
15	We regularly honor and recognize our employees and their contributions.	⑤ ③ ② ① ⓪

Innovate as a Habit   **Your Rating**

16	We honor and respect failure and use it for coaching purposes.	⑤ ③ ② ① ⓪
17	We teach our employees how to be creative.	⑤ ③ ② ① ⓪
18	We enable our employees to work on what excites them most.	⑤ ③ ② ① ⓪
19	We teach our employees the best ways to collaborate.	⑤ ③ ② ① ⓪
20	We encourage employees to challenge the status quo and recognize them for doing so.	⑤ ③ ② ① ⓪

Make Work Meaningful   **Your Rating**

| 21 | Managers collaborate with their employees to set SMART goals. | ⑤ ③ ② ① ⓪ |
| 22 | Our managers and leaders actively help employees build meaningful careers. | ⑤ ③ ② ① ⓪ |

23	We coach and mentor our people to be self-aware and have purpose in work and life.	⑤ ③ ② ① ⓪
24	We deploy a buddy system to help employees do well in their current and future jobs.	⑤ ③ ② ① ⓪
25	We enable job rotations, international assignments and on-the-job learning and training.	⑤ ③ ② ① ⓪

How does your organization stack up?

Use the following scoring guide to assess how your organization stacks up in creating a Potluck Culture.

<u>Note</u>: Reliability and validity tests have not been conducted on this assessment. It is merely suggested as a guide to build interest and awareness of the various people initiatives your organization can undertake to enhance its organizational and strategic imperatives.

Add up the rating numbers for each question to determine total points. (Maximum 125 points)

105–125 points: Congratulations!

Your organization appears to have a high level of commitment to employees and a Potluck Culture. Supporting authentic people practices is a norm in the organization. This level suggests the following:

- There is a strategy in place for managing people, building a people-centric culture and strategic talent management.

- The organization recognizes people as essential to productivity and profitability.

- Supportive, positive, and respectful people-centric practices are integrated into most aspects of the organization.

85–104 points: You're well on your way!

Your organization has a strong commitment to creating a Potluck Culture and improving employee engagement. This level suggests the following:

- Several initiatives are in place to support a people-centric culture.

- A focus on people is being considered in many areas.

- People-centric initiatives are being incorporated into many aspects of the organization.

65–84 points: Not bad…a good start!

Your organization recognizes the importance of a Potluck Culture and is making an effort to develop and support it.

Less than 65 points: OK…let's get started!

Your organization has room to improve, but you've already started the process by filling out this form. Now is the perfect time to begin efforts to improve your organizational culture.

Next Steps

Now that you have identified areas of opportunity within your organization to better support a healthy workplace, the next step is to integrate this information into a work plan. This will help form the basis for developing a comprehensive strategy for improved organizational health and performance.

Dr. Ranjit Nair Ph.D. is available to help you with

- consultation on incorporating a Potluck Culture and integrate it with your strategic business plan,

- building a Strategic Talent Strategy and Succession Plan,

- developing business, individual and organizational stories to enhance your company's brand around a People vison,

- developing communication collateral to demonstrate the importance of a reverence for people,

- building a meaningful Total Rewards Strategy,

- providing educational materials on a variety of HR topics, and

- providing on-site presentations on a variety of talent, leadership and human capital management topics.

Contact Dr. Nair at potluckculture.com, ranjitnairphd.com, or ranjit@price-associates.com.

Appendix B

NEW LEADER
ASSIMILATION TEMPLATE

Company Logo Here

Employee Name
Title
Function

New Leader Assimilation Plan

"Accelerating the Success of New Leaders"
(Tagline typically used by the company to motivate leaders)

Employee/Leader
Title
Function/Department
Assimilation Plan
Date

Objectives

- Accelerate successful orientation to Company X's ABC (e.g., marketing) function

- Establish credibility and steadily accelerate ability to deliver results

- Swiftly transition into the organization with ease and clarity, with minimal downtime and disruption to client needs/deliverables

- Accelerate understanding of key initiatives, business goals, and challenges (strategies, priorities, and performance plans)

- Accelerate business performance

- Build key relationships essential for future success

- Clarify short- and medium-term objectives

- Enhance understanding of aspects of Company X's business and culture

- Provide support through feedback, coaching and follow-up

- Establish clear understanding of objectives and expectations from supervisor and teammates

- Establish and articulate individual goals for FY 20XX

Onboarding Plan Steps

1. **Define Assimilation Plan and Objectives:** Manager reviews the Onboarding Plan and timeline and introduces key team members and stakeholders. Manager also helps me to hone and

develop 30-, 60-, 90-, and 180-day goals and review the opportunities and challenges of new role.

2. **Build Key Relationships:** Meet with support partners and team members to learn about current and future initiatives. Meet individually, and as a team, with direct reports to share my philosophy and expectations and agree on goals and priorities. Meet with peer team members to develop effective working relationships.

3. **Learn the Business, Organization, and Culture:** Read relevant materials and complete required training. Familiarize myself with the company's organizational structure by networking both within and outside of my function and with business units/regions across the organization. Review organization charts as appropriate and if available.

4. **Establish Self as Leader and Business Partner:** Focus on strategy and key business issues. Determine the biggest risks/threats to the organization and the Human Resources department. Define key growth opportunities for the business. Collaborate with business partners to establish what is working or is not working. Participate in "Key Stakeholder Review" meetings and processes beginning around the thirty-day mark.

5. **Deliver Results**

Objectives	Week One	30–60 Days	90 Days	120 Days	180+ Days
1. Define assimilation plan and individual objectives	●———	●			
2. Build key relationships	●———	———	→		
3. Learn the business, organization and culture		●———	———	●	
4. Establish self as leader and business partner			●———	●	
5. Deliver results		●———	———	———	→

Appendix C

NEW EMPLOYEE ASSIMILATION

New Employee Name
Manager Checklist

_____ Company history, leaders (past and present), customers, performance, and financials

_____ Vision, culture, and work environment

_____ Leadership organization chart; how company is structured and organized

_____ Key business areas, functions, regions and locations; products and technologies

_____ Affiliation and relationship with other organizations; position in market

_____ Performance management process—(goal-setting conversation must be completed within the first month of employment)

_____ Eligible compensation and benefits conversation; salary review process

_____ Other rewards of work; training and development activities; talent management

_____ Work culture expectations; key policies

_____ Safety orientation and training information

_____ Safety orientation; logistics, computer equipment, business cards, and floor maps

_____ Team orientation

_____   _____

Manager's Name   Date Completed

Appendix D

HOW TO DEVELOP SMART GOALS

What gets measured ultimately gets done. Goals serve as the basis for performance assessment discussions, and the goal-setting process clarifies expectations and priorities. Individual goals that link to the department or function ensure that the "bigger picture" needs of an organization are being met. If employees can understand and see the big picture, this is nirvana. All employees—especially high performers—want to know how their actions impact the company.

The formal performance management process touches upon major challenges and initiatives faced by the company and the unit where the employees work. The conversation between the manager and employees should go into detail not just on the *what*, but also the *how* of the goals. In other words, both the results of the goals and the behaviors that inspire them matter equally. How individuals influence outcomes and contribute to the overall success of their organization is of vital importance.

Why do we need to set goals?

- Goals provide a clear idea of what needs to be achieved.
- Employees and managers can plan what needs to be done to achieve these goals through time, resources, and relationships.

- Goals allow for the measurement of progress and what efforts need to be enhanced, modified, or even reset as deadlines approach.

Here are examples of goals to set:

- Increase profits, customer satisfaction, sales, and effectiveness.
- Make products, services, or an image.
- Improve processes, results, or relationships.
- Reduce risk, expenses, or competition.
- Save time, money, space, or energy.

What, then, are SMART goals and how do we set them?

SMART goals must have specific, focused criteria, so they can be easily interpreted and accomplished.

(S) Specific—Detail the exact level of performance expected of the employees.

(M) Measurable—Present goals that can be observed and measured as employees progress.

(A) Attainable—Establish realistic criteria. Goals should challenge employees to do their best but also be achievable or else the employees will be disillusioned and withdraw or become apathetic.

(R) Relevant—Develop goals that pertain directly to the performance challenge being managed.

(T) Time frame—Provide deadlines to help people work harder to get a task completed.

Examples of SMART goals:

Example #1

Organizational process for a new product/service introduction

- Ineffective goal: Introduce new (product/service)
- Effective goal: Introduce four new (products/services) by (month/year)

Example #2

Organizational process for customer service

- Ineffective goal: Maximize customer satisfaction in (product/service) by (month/year)
- Effective goal: Increase customer satisfaction ratings to 90% in (product/service) by the end of (month/year)

Here are tips on choosing effective wording for SMART goals in performance conversations:

1. Choose a verb: increase, decrease, reduce, improve, deliver, or grow
2. Define the objective: what you wish or will work toward to improve
3. Identify how much: target goals and what success looks like
4. Identify by when: time frame for completion of goal
5. Create a link: connection between your objectives and those of your company

Here are some questions to ask to help refine performance goals:

1. What is the current challenge?
2. What outcomes would indicate success by meeting this challenge?

3. Who are the constituents affected by this challenge?

4. What metrics make the most sense for this area?

5. What are our company values?

6. How am I expected to behave?

7. How do I stay true to my company's culture?

8. Why are these my goals?

ENDNOTES

Chapter 2

1.   "2014 Trends in Global Employee Engagement," *Aon*, accessed May 14, 2015, http://www.aon.com/human-capital-consulting/ thought-leadership/talent_mgmt/2014-trends-in-global-employ- ee-engagement.jsp.

2.   Jeff Schwartz, Josh Bersin, and Bill Pelster, "Global Human Capital Trends 2014: Engaging the 21st-Century Workforce" *Deloitte*, March 7, 2014, http://www2.deloitte.com/global/en/ pages/human-capital/articles/human-capital-trends-2014.html; Josh Bersin, Dimple Agarwal, Bill Pelster, and Jeff Schwartz, "Global Human Capital Trends 2015: Leading in the New World of Work," *Deloitte*, February 27, 2015, http://www2. deloitte.com/au/en/pages/human-capital/articles/introduction- human-capital-trends.html.

3.   Dan Bursch and Kip Kelly, "Talent Management: Managing the Multigenerational Workplace," *Executive Development Blog, University of North Carolina, Kenan-Flagler Business School*, posted on May 8, 2014, http://execdev.kenan-flagler.unc.edu/ blog/managing-the-multigenerational-workplace-0.

4. Ron Price and Randy Lisk, *The Complete Leader: Everything You Need to Become a High-Performing Leader* (Eagle, Idaho: Aloha Publishing, 2014).

5. Mitra Toossi, "Employment Outlook: 2010–2020: Labor Force Projections to 2020—A More Slowly Growing Workforce," US Department of Labor, updated February 21, 2012, http://www.bls.gov/opub/mlr/2012/01/art3full.pdf.

6. Jessica Brack, "Maximizing Millennials in the Workplace," *Executive Development Blog, University of North Carolina, Kenan-Flagler Business School,* posted on November 26, 2014, http://execdev.kenan-flagler.unc.edu/blog/maximizing-millennials-in-the-workplace.

7. Schwartz, Bersin, and Pelster, "Engaging the 21st-Century Workforce"; Bersin, Agarwal, Pelster, and Schwartz, "Leading in the New World of Work."

8. Bursch and Kelly, "Talent Management"; Brack, "Maximizing Millennials."

9. Nora Wu, Julie Gordon, Anne Donovan and Julia Sheasby, "Engaging and Empowering Millennials," PriceWaterhouseCoopers, December 5, 2014, http://www.pwc.com/gx/en/hr-management-services/publications/assets/pwc-engaging-and-empowering-millennials.pdf.

10. Schwartz, Bersin, and Pelster, "Engaging the 21st-Century Workforce"; Bersin, Agarwal, Pelster, and Schwartz, "Leading in the New World of Work"; Wu, Gordon, Donovan, and Sheasby, "Engaging and Empowering Millennials."

11. Ibid.

12. "Millennials in Adulthood: Detached from Institutions, Networked with Friends," *Pew Research Center*, March

7, 2014, http://www.pewsocialtrends.org/2014/03/07/
millennials-in-adulthood/.

13. Wu, Gordon, Donovan, and Sheasby, "Engaging and
Empowering Millennials."

14. "Millennials in Adulthood"; Bursch and Kelly, "Talent Management."

15. Ibid.

16. "How Millennials Get News: Inside the Habits of America's
First Digital Generation," *American Press Institute*, March 16,
2015, http://www.americanpressinstitute.org/publications/
reports/survey-research/millennials-news/.

Chapter 3

1. "The 2014 Global Workforce Study: Driving Engagement
through a Consumer-Like Experience," *Towers Watson*,
August 2014, http://www.towerswatson.com/en-US/
Insights/IC-Types/Survey-Research-Results/2014/08/
the-2014-global-workforce-study.

2. Wu, Gordon, Donovan, and Sheasby, "Engaging and
Empowering Millennials."

3. Bursch and Kelly, "Talent Management."

4. Ibid.

5. Schwartz, Bersin, and Pelster, "Engaging the 21st-Century
Workforce."

6. "Millennials in Adulthood."

7. Bursch and Kelly, "Talent Management."

8. Lisa Gevelber, "The Shift to Constant Connectivity," *Google Think Insights*, May 2013, http://www.google.com.au/think/articles/shift-to-constant-connectivity.html.

9. Bersin, Agarwal, Pelster, and Schwartz, "Leading in the New World of Work."

10. "Millennials in Adulthood."

Chapter 4

1. Voltaire, *BrainyQuote.com*, accessed May 14, 2015, http://www.brainyquote.com/quotes/quotes/v/voltaire109645.html.

Chapter 5

1. "2014 Global Workforce Study."

2. T. M. Amabile, B. A. Hennessey and B. S. Grossman, "Social Influences on Creativity: The Effects of Contracted-For Reward," *Journal of Personality and Social Psychology* 50, no. 1 (January 1986): 14–23.

3. Ibid.

Chapter 6

1. Aristotle, *BrainyQuote.com*, accessed May 14, 2015, http://www.brainyquote.com/quotes/quotes/a/aristotle145967.html.

2. Tim Brown, "How Do You Build a Culture of Innovation?" *Yale Insights*, accessed May 14, 2015, http://insights.som.yale.edu/insights/how-do-you-build-culture-innovation.

3. Steve Jobs, *Goodreads.com,* accessed May 14, 2015, http://
    www.goodreads.com/quotes/622900-my-model-for-business-
    is-the-beatles-they-were-four.

4. Soren Kaplan, "Six Ways to Create a Culture of Innovation,"
    Fast Company, December 21, 2013, http://www.fastcodesign.
    com/1672718/6-ways-to-create-a-culture-of-innovation.

5. Polly LaBarre , "What It Takes to Do New Things at
    Work, Overnight," *Fortune,* March 22, 2012,
    http://fortune.com/2012/03/22/what-it-takes-to-do-
    new-things-at-work-overnight/.

6. Jeff Zias, "How 'Doing Your Own Thing' Gets Innovation
    Moving," *Intuit Network,* January 20, 2012, http://network.
    intuit.com/2012/01/20/how-%E2%80%98doing-your-own-
    thing%E2%80%99-gets-innovation-moving/.

7. Max Nisen, "17 of the Most Mysterious Corporate Labs,"
    Business Insider, February 19, 2013, http://www.businessin-
    sider.com/coolest-skunk-works-2013-2.

8. John Cleese, Gurteen.com, accessed May 14, 2015, http://
    www.gurteen.com/gurteen/gurteen.nsf/id/L004957/.

9. Collen Taylor, "Google Co-Founders Talk Regulation,
    Innovation, and More in Fireside Chat with Vinod Khosla," *Tech
    Crunch,* July 16, 2014, http://techcrunch.com/2014/07/06/
    google-co-founders-talk-long-term-innovation-making-big-bets-
    and-more-in-fireside-chat-with-vinod-khosla/.

10. Howard Baldwin, "Time Off to Innovate: Good Idea or a Waste
    of Tech Talent?" *ComputerWorld,* July 24, 2012, http://www.
    computerworld.com/article/2506129/it-management/time-off-
    to-innovate--good-idea-or-a-waste-of-tech-talent-.html.

11. Ibid.

12. Daniel Pink, "How to Deliver Innovation Overnight," *Daniel H. Pink*, accessed May 14, 2015, http://www.danpink.com/2011/07/how-to-deliver-innovation-overnight/.

Chapter 7

1. "Our New Name," CVS Health, accessed May 14, 2015, http://www.cvshealth.com/research-insights/health-topics/our-new-name.

2. "Name Change," Domino's TV Spot, ispot.tv, aired May 8, 2015, http://www.ispot.tv/ad/7xnm/dominos-name-change.

3. Stacy Lamy, "Sriracha Sauce: A Love Story," Guardian Liberty Voice, May 12, 2014, http://guardianlv.com/2014/05/sriracha-sauce-a-love-story/.

Chapter 8

1. Vineet Nayar, *Employees First, Customers Second: Turning Conventional Management Upside Down* (Watertown, MA: Harvard Business Review Press, 2010).

2. "Changing the DNA of Cancer Care," You Tube video, posted September 16, 2014, https://www.youtube.com/watch?v=hhjkkjirr-g.

3. Oscar Raymundo, "Richard Branson: Companies Should Put Employees First," *Inc.*, October 28, 2014, http://www.inc.com/oscar-raymundo/richard-branson-companies-should-put-employees-first.html.

4. Ibid.

5. Ibid.

ACKNOWLEDGMENTS

This is a book about Leadership. Specifically, it is about leaders recognizing the critical importance of organizational culture in driving business success. People want to know what type of team they are joining and who the leaders are and, most importantly, how they are treated. This is *all* about culture.

While there is universal agreement that organizational culture, first, does indeed exist, and, second, plays a fundamental and vital role in how people behave, how leaders lead and organize, and how they drive and motivate their people, there is little consensus on what exactly organizational culture is. One thing that is certain is that it's *all about People!*

All organizations do, indeed, have discernable cultures whether they are implicitly implemented or manifested on their own. Cultures can also shift based on who the leaders are in the company or what the competitive stakes they face or where their organizations are in the life cycle. Cultures, of course, are about rituals, unwritten rules, artifacts, beliefs, symbols, colors, and also expected behavior. These elements can change, but one constant that will never change is that People will always adorn any company!

So, this book is about People and what their organizations can do to revere them and build a culture of respect, dialogue, and reverence around them with the ultimate goal to leverage this people-driven culture as the most formidable asset needed to win in today's competitive landscape.

Organizational culture was first "discovered" in the late 1980s by stalwart management scientists such as Dr. Edgar Schein, Dr. Geert Hofstede, and Dr. Andrew Brown, but it wasn't until the last twenty years that the link between culture and performance was established. I first realized the link almost serendipitously. When I first assumed a leadership role, I realized that people yearn for a lot of things and this includes elements that their work worlds offer. They spend so much of their time at work and, many times, bring that work home, so to speak. Therefore, for this reason alone, it is imperative and crucial that organizational leaders start to respect, honor, and venerate them in authentic and genuine ways if they want to keep their organizations successful.

Potluck Culture: Five Strategies to Engage the Modern Workplace would not have been possible without the aforementioned realization. The book, itself, would not have been possible without the help—directly or indirectly—from a whole host of people that I had the pleasure and honor of being associated with. I try, respectfully, to identify some of these individuals below.

Dr. Thomas Sechrest, Associate Professor and Director of the Master of Science in Leadership and Change at the Bill Munday School of Management and Business, St. Edward's University Austin, TX

Tom inspired me to pursue a desire to become a management scientist and pursue a Ph.D. He also is a great friend and my former Dean at St. Edward's University. He is a great conversationalist and expert in Leadership and Management and, through our enlightening dialogue over the years, helped me to deeply understand how leaders learn and how they are developed.

ACKNOWLEDGMENTS

Dr. Stanley Horner, Associate Professor of Management, Austin, TX

Stan is also a great friend and my former boss at St. Edward's University. He was instrumental in taking a chance on me—a corporate suit—to delve into the world of academia and try my hand at teaching. I'd like to think that I was somewhat successful. Stan taught me a great deal about self-awareness. He let me "do my thing" with the courses I taught, and I injected a lot of what's in this book for my students at St. Ed's.

Tom Cross, Partner (retired) at PriceWaterhouseCoopers, FL

Tom was my former boss, and I want to thank him for giving me my first opportunity in human resource management and helping me to find my calling. It started in 1997 and changed my career—and life—forever. He believed that I had a way with people and that I knew how to make the link between what they do and what our customers wanted.

Dr. Bijan Masumian (Learning and Development Manager) and **Dr. Farnaz Masumian**, (author of *The Divine Art of Meditation*), Austin, TX

I wish to thank my dear friends the Masumians for showing me what it means to demonstrate the ultimate appreciation and unfettered love and respect for people—all people. They taught me that goodness in people is part of the DNA of all humans, and if we could all tap into some of that goodness on a regular basis, the world would be a better place. They also taught me how to meditate—a practice that certainly has a place in the modern workplace.

Former workplace colleagues

I also thank all of my staff and teammates and supervisors at the various corporations I was a part of for their support, high performance and commitment to excellence, and putting up with me and, most of all, in revering people and helping me build winning, high-performance cultures.

Jiji Nair, M.S. Nutrition and Wellness Coach

Jiji is my wife and partner of the last twenty years. She is my best friend and taught me a great deal about many things. She is the consummate relationship builder. Always bright, positive, happy, and smiling, she has been instrumental in teaching me to appreciate food, potluck gatherings, and encouraging me to cook and make dishes and share them with others. I don't know if *Potluck Culture* would be written without her by my side.

Nikhil Nair and Nikita Nair

My children, Nicky and Nikita, are awesome! They've never been a burden, have truly put up with me, held the fort down at home when I was away traveling, have taken care of their mother and can always be counted on to do the right thing. I am especially proud of them for always respecting people, especially the older generation, and always looking to learn from them and respectfully having conversations with them. My children have never shied away from having meaningful dialogue with anyone—young or old—and they are the true champions of my heart and life.

Aloha Publishing, Boise, ID

My deepest thanks goes to Maryanna Young of Aloha Publishing and her team of capable cohorts. Kim Foster's expert editing, Jennifer Regner's suggestions, and Stacy Ennis' encouragement to me to tell my true stories all made this book become a reality. I wish to thank them deeply and humbly for making me a first-time author—a dream come true.

ACKNOWLEDGMENTS

Ziggy Nair, my best friend

This may seem odd to some, but I owe a lot to Ziggy, my dog. He—a labradoodle—is my best friend and always listens to me and has changed my family's lives forever. Of course, Ziggy thinks he's human (or he thinks *we're* dogs!) and has the run of our home. He takes me for a long walk every morning, and we play ball together a lot. I never realized how much I enjoyed playing and now I have him as well as my children to play with. Yes, they're adults but we should never stop playing! It was during one of those play sessions with Ziggy that I had the courage to sit down and write *Potluck Culture*.